CHRISTIAN SOLDIER

SPIRITUAL WARFARE

LESLIE M. JOHN

Put on the whole armour of God, that ye may be able to stand against the wiles of the devil. For we wrestle not against flesh and blood, but against principalities, against powers, against the rulers of the darkness of this world, against spiritual wickedness in high places. (Ephesians 6:11-12)

CHRISTIAN SOLDIER

SPIRITUAL WARFARE

LESLIE M. JOHN

Copyright © Leslie M. John 2013 All Rights Reserved

No part of this book may be reproduced or transmitted in any form or by any means, electronic or mechanical, including photocopying, recording, or by any information storage and retrieval system, without permission in writing from the copyright owner, Leslie M. John.

The entire text in this book is deposited with Library of Congress Copyright Office, 101 Independence Avenue, SE Washington, DC 20559-6000, USA. This work is protected by Law in US; and internationally, according to The Berne Convention 1971

All Scriptures are taken from KJV from open domain

ISBN-10:0-9890283-3-X
ISBN-13:978-0-9890283-3-2

Table of Contents

CHRISTIAN SOLDIER 1
PREFACE 7
INTRODUCTION 10
CHAPTER 1 THE ARMOUR OF GOD 14
    JESUS THWARTS PRESUPPOSITIONS.................19
    THE JUDGES AND THE JUDGMENTS.................34
CHAPTER 2 TRUTH 38
    FALSE PROPHETS 41
CHAPTER 3. RIGHTEOUNESS 48
    DEAD IN TRESPASSES 49
    THE GOSPEL OF PEACE..................................55
    PEACE FROM THE SON OF GOD 56
CHAPTER 4 FORGIVENESS FROM SON OF MAN.62
    THE SON OF MAN...62
    THE POWER TO FORGIVE SINS.......................63
    SALVATION IS THE GIFT OF GOD......................65
CHAPTER 5 SHIELD OF FAITH 67
    LAW AND GRACE 69
CHAPTER 6 HELMET OF SALVATION 85
    OUR SALVATION IS SECURE.............................86
    THE LOVE OF GOD 87

SALVATION IS THE GIFT OF GOD 91
WHAT DOES HANDING OVER TO SATAN MEAN? 94
THE SEVERITY OF JUDGMENT 95
THE FEAST OF ATONEMENT 97
HIS PRECIOUS BLOOD 101
CHPATER 7 SWORD OF THE SPIRIT 106
THE DEVIL TEMPTS LORD JESUS 107
CHAPTER 8 PRAYER 113
SACRIFICES 116
GOD DELIVERS US FROM CURSE 121
VENGEANCE BELONGS TO GOD 123
CHAPTER 9 THE PRAYER OF JESUS 127
JESUS DIED IN OUR STEAD 130
CHAPTER 10　WE PREACH CHRIST CRUCIFIED 135
CAN WE CONFINE GOD TO A PLACE? 137
HUMILITY 140
PROPITIATION 143
REDEMPTION 144
THE LOVE OF GOD 146
JUSTIFICATION 152
RECONCILIATION 157
EYE OF A NEEDLE 159

CHAPTER 11 THE RISEN LORD ASCENDED..........171
   FORGIVING ONE ANOTHER 174
CHAPTER 12 REPLIES BY ADAM AND CAIN 178
   ADAM'S REPLY 178
   CAIN'S REPLY: 179
   GOD SAID..179
   'FUGITIVE' 180
   'VAGABOND'..181
CHAPTER 13   CAIN AND HIS CURSE...................182
   WHERE DID CAIN GET HIS WIFE FROM? 187
CHAPTER 14 STREET OF GOLD 192
   MOSES WARNED 199

PREFACE

My mission is to proclaim the good news of our Lord Jesus Christ as revealed to me through Holy Bible and from various teachers, preachers, and commentators. This is my voluntary service to God in the name of His only begotten Son Lord Jesus Christ.

I share the truth of knowledge of God with others with good intention of bringing them to the knowledge of the living God, the God of Abraham, the God of Isaac, the God of Jacob, and the Father of our Lord Jesus Christ. My mission is to proclaim the Gospel of Lord Jesus Christ and not converting forcibly anyone to Christianity. One may accept or reject any or part of my writings/teachings.   No offense is meant to any individual or any religion or any organization. Please visit http://www.lesliejohn.net/

I pray for the peace of Jerusalem and desire that all Jews may accept Lord Jesus as their personal Savior and Messiah.

"Pray for the peace of Jerusalem: they shall prosper that love thee" (Psalms 122:6)

I firmly believe in the saying of Jesus, who said:

"No man can come to me, except the Father which hath sent me draw him: and I will raise him up at the last day" John 6:44.

My efforts to teach or preach are of no use unless Lord Jesus Christ Himself intervenes and the Father draws a person unto Him.

Description:

We wrestle with principalities and against powers, against the rulers of the darkness of this world, against spiritual wickedness in high places and, therefore, we should always seek the power from Lord Jesus Christ to overcome them. We should, therefore, stand with our loins girt ever ready to fight these evil forces with the help of help and in the name of Lord Jesus Christ, who defeated Satan at the cross.

The principalities and powers are superhuman devilish agencies and demonic powers as we read in Romans 8:38 Ephesians 3:10; Ephesians 6:12 Colossians 1:16; Colossians 2:10, 15.   We must know our enemy. Our enemy is not any man in his flesh but the devil, the Old Dragon that deceived Eve in the Garden of Eden. Satan is defeated foe but still alive with his limited power ever casting doubts in the minds of believers in Christ.

This book explains the weapons of war that a believer has to put on to be successful in the combat against the evil forces from Satan, temptations from him, and subdue him in the battle against him.

INTRODUCTION

Ever since Satan deceived Adam and Eve, man has been struggling to overcome the temptations from Satan, whose weapon against man had always been deceptive, causing doubts, fear, and uncertainty. His weapon in the form of a familiar question "Yea, hath God said" poses serious doubts in the minds of people. Satan never ceases to ask that question over and over again. The phrase "Yea, hath God said"...causes confusions and doubts about God, and many became his followers because they did not depend on God to find a resolution to the question. It is not possible to have victory over Satan unless we depend on Lord Jesus Christ and put on weapons of spiritual warfare.

Apostle Paul writes:

There hath no temptation taken you but such as is common to man: but God is faithful, who will not suffer you to be tempted above that ye are able; but will with the temptation also make a way to escape, that ye may be able to bear it. (1 Corinthians 10:13)

God blessed man and gave him authority over the fish of the sea, over the fowl of the air, and every living that moves upon the earth. All that He said to man was to be fruitful, multiply and replenish the earth, and subdue it. It was God's blessing, and He undertook to support man whenever he faced any threat. .

In six days He created heavens, earth, and all the host of them, and all His work of creation ended on the sixth day. He rested on the seventh day. He created man and woman on the sixth day and talked to them on the same day. Woman was not created on the eighth day, as some humorously say that she was created on the eight day, and ever since God had no rest. No; His creation ended on the sixth day.

The LORD God formed man from the dust of the ground, and breathed His breath into man's nostrils, and when God's breath entered into man, he became a living soul. Until God breathed His breath into the nostrils of man, he was mere lump of dust, made into a form that looked like man. Man had no life before God breathed His life into man's nostrils. When that breath stops in man he is said to be dead.

Will man be really dead in body, soul and spirit, when the breath of God leaves man? No, only the physical body, which was made from dust, becomes useless and returns to dust. The soul is comforted "Hades"; of those who are saved way away from those who are unsaved. The spirit returns to God because it belongs to God rented to be in the bodies of men and animals.

When the Lord comes again the dead in Christ will rise to life with their glorified bodies and those who are living will be caught to be with the Lord for ever and ever. However, the unsaved will remain in the grave waiting to rise for the final judgment at the "Great white throne" and to be case in the "Lake of Fire".

For the Lord himself shall descend from heaven with a shout, with the voice of the archangel, and with the trump of God: and the dead in Christ shall rise first: Then we which are alive and remain shall be caught up together with them in the clouds, to meet the Lord in the air: and so shall we ever be with the Lord. (1 Thessalonians 4:16-17)

The death entered into the world because man sinned and there is resurrection of the dead. Those who accept Lord Jesus Christ as their Savior, receive salvation by confessing their sins to Him, and believe that God raised Him from the dead. They are never dead but sleep in the Lord until their bodies are raised incorruptible on His second coming.

The first man to die on this earth was Abel and when his spirit left him it cried unto the Lord of the offence he faced from his own brother, Cain. Cain never repented of his sin.

Lord Jesus Christ's blood was greater than Abel and it cried unto the Father of the offence that man has done to Him, who was the Son of God, came down into this world in the form of servant, and in the likeness of man.

And the LORD God formed man of the dust of the ground, and breathed into his nostrils the breath of life; and man became a living soul. (Genesis 2:7)

He blessed the seventh day, and sanctified it and because He rested on the seventh day from all His work he sanctified the seventh day. God saw everything He created was very good. Evening and morning were counted as one day, and when He saw that His creation was very good, it was the end of sixth day.

And God blessed them, and God said unto them, Be fruitful, and multiply, and replenish the earth, and subdue it: and have dominion over the fish of the sea, and over the fowl of the air, and over every living thing that moveth upon the earth. (Genesis 1:28)

CHAPTER 1
THE ARMOUR OF GOD

For though we walk in the flesh, we do not war after the flesh: (For the weapons of our warfare are not carnal, but mighty through God to the pulling down of strong holds. (2 Corinthians 10:3-4)

Apostle Paul exhorted the brethren to be strong in the Lord taking refuge in the mighty Lord's power and seeking them to put on the whole armor of God in order that they may fight against fleshly desires caused by the devil. This devil is the one that deceived Eve and his subtle question "Yea hath God said?" is never ending.

We wrestle with principalities and against powers, against the rulers of the darkness of this world, against spiritual wickedness in high places and, therefore, we should always seek the power from Lord Jesus Christ to overcome them. We should, therefore, stand with our loins girt ever ready to fight these evil forces with the help of help and in the name of Lord Jesus Christ, who defeated Satan at the cross.

The principalities and powers are superhuman devilish agencies and demonic powers as we read in Romans 8:38 Ephesians 3:10; Ephesians 6:12 Colossians 1:16; Colossians 2:10, 15.   We must know our enemy. Our enemy is not any man in his flesh but the devil, the Old Dragon that deceived Eve in the Garden of Eden. Satan is defeated foe but still alive with his limited power ever casting doubts in the minds of believers in Christ.

Now the serpent was more subtil than any beast of the field which the LORD God had made. And he said unto the woman, Yea, hath God said, Ye shall not eat of every tree of the garden? (Genesis 3:1)

Satan' usage of this phrase "Yea, hath God said"...to cast doubts and tempt the believers in Christ is his very strong weapon to deceive and drift away from God. Satan is the adversary of man and unless man takes refuge in Lord Jesus Christ to help him out from the deceptive ways and temptations of that dragon man in his capacity is no match to Satan.   It is like man trying hitting and knocking down a mountain to with his feeble fist. Unless man has the power-filled fist of power like dynamite he would not be able to knock down Satan.

Apostle Paul realized this in his ministry and strongly suggested that we should have the full set of armor to and attack it with the sword to defeat it. The weapons of war that a believer needs to put on are:

1) TRUTH
2) RIGHTEOUNESS
3) THE GOSPEL OF PEACE
4) SHIELD OF FAITH
5) HELMET OF SALVATION
6) SWORD OF THE SPIRIT

"For the word of God is quick, and powerful, and sharper than any two-edged sword, piercing even to the dividing asunder of soul and spirit, and of the joints and marrow, and is a discerner of the thoughts and intents of the heart" (Hebrews 4:12)

There is comfort in the words of Lord Jesus Christ who said...

"And I give unto them eternal life; and they shall never perish, neither shall any man pluck them out of my hand" (John 10:28)

Such love and protection as promised by Lord Jesus is unfathomable by any man. Apostle Paul bowed on his knees and sought in prayer that the Father of our Lord Jesus Christ may grant riches of His glory to those in Ephesus Church, and to as well in order that the inner man in them and in us may be strengthened. (Ephesians 3:14-21, 1Timothy 3:16-17)

Apostle Paul desired that Christ may dwell in believers in Christ and inasmuch as believers in Christ are rooted and grounded in love, should be able to praise Christ's love the depth of which is unfathomable, the height, breadth, and length cannot be measured. It surpasses any one's understanding and knowledge and that we may be filled with the fullness of God. The Lord is able to keep us from falling and do give us more than we think or ask. He protects us from falling and may the never ceasing glory be unto Him throughout all ages.   (cf. Ephesians 3:14-21)

A born-again child faces many struggles in this world, especially from the temptations that Satan brings but the believer in Christ can be triumphant over such wile desires that this world offers.   One of the three temptations that Lord Jesus Christ has successfully overcome was by answering the devil from the written word of God. To live in this world is spiritual warfare for believers in Christ every day with that Old Dragon, the devil that deceived Eve in the Garden of Eden. To be triumphant the believers in Christ need the strength in Lord Jesus Christ.

Put on the whole armour of God, that ye may be able to stand against the wiles of the devil. For we wrestle not against flesh and blood, but against principalities, against powers, against the rulers of the darkness of this world, against spiritual wickedness in high places. Wherefore take unto you the whole armour of God, that ye may be able to withstand in the evil day, and having done all, to stand. Stand therefore, having your loins girt about with truth, and having on the breastplate of righteousness; And your feet shod with the preparation of the gospel of peace; Above all, taking the shield of faith, wherewith ye shall be able to quench all the fiery darts of the wicked. And take the helmet of salvation, and the sword of the Spirit, which is the word of God: Praying always with all prayer and supplication in the Spirit, and watching thereunto with all perseverance and supplication for all saints; (Ephesians 6:11-18)

When Apostle Paul was in prison in Rome he was closely guarded by Roman Soldier. The duty of Roman soldier is to make sure that the prisoner does not run away from the prison cell and become a threat to the emperor.

Every once in a while after few scheduled hours Roman soldiers take turn to guard the prisoner. This arrangement helped Paul to preach the Gospel to the soldiers.

In turn, Paul also learnt from them very impressive facts about protective pieces of armor that they wore in order that they may not get hurt. Paul closely observed the pieces of protective items and learnt and taught spiritual lessons in his epistle to Ephesians Chapter 6.

It is imperative that we recognize who our enemy is and he is without any doubt Satan, the Old Dragon, who deceived our first parents in the Garden of Eden.   Satan's war against Christians is never ceasing and, therefore, a Christian needs to necessarily have the weapons of war as described in Ephesians 6:11-18 in order to defeat Satan and stand firm in the Lord.   The protective pieces in all constitute Lord Jesus Christ, and when we put on Jesus we are sure to win our common enemy who is the adversary, the Satan.

For as many of you as have been baptized into Christ have put on Christ. (Galatians 3:27)

Be sober, be vigilant; because your adversary the devil, as a roaring lion, walketh about, seeking whom he may devour: (1 Peter 5:8)

JESUS THWARTS PRESUPPOSITIONS

"Jesus answered them, Is it not written in your law, I said, Ye are gods? If he called them gods,

unto whom the word of God came, and the scripture cannot be broken; Say ye of him, whom the Father hath sanctified, and sent into the world, Thou blasphemest; because I said, I am the Son of God?" (John 10:34-36)

John Chapter 10 shows us great deal of truth concerning Lord Jesus Christ, the Son of God: *"Who, being in the form of God, thought it not robbery to be equal with God: But made himself of no reputation, and took upon him the form of a servant, and was made in the likeness of men" (Philippians 2:6-7)*

In John Chapter 9 and 10 there is narration of a sequence of events that eventually show that Jesus is the Son of God, and He is the Very God Himself.

Jesus said:

1. He is the Good shepherd

2. Sheep hear his voice

3. Good shepherd knows His sheep

4. His sheep know that He is the Good Shepherd

5. Good shepherd protects His sheep

6. His Father gave Him the sheep and no man can pluck them out of His Father's hand

7. Jesus and the Father are ONE

The Jews then took up stones to stone him. This is the context where Jesus quoted Psalm 82 to shake the foundation of the knowledge of Pharisees and Rabbis.

In John Chapter 9 there is narration of how a blind man was healed by Lord Jesus Christ and the blind man believed Him as the Son of God and worshipped him. Pharisees, who always tried to trap Jesus on some point argued with Him many times.

When they questioned Jesus about their own condition as to whether they were blind, Jesus said to them, that He came to give sight to the blind that they may see and also make blind some like those Pharisees who see yet do not understand. Jesus said if they were blind there would not have been sin upon them but their sin remains on them because they claim that they see; but Jesus knew that they did not perceive Him or His works.

The reason why Jews took up stones to stone Jesus was that Jesus claimed to be God. Jesus said He and the Father are one. Jesus claimed that He came from the Father and He did the works of the Father. The Jews thought that Jesus was blaspheming God. Although God manifested Himself as Triune God "Jehovah" is one. The Father, The Son, and the Holy Spirit are three in one and are co-equal, co-existent but have different function to perform, yet all the Three are One.

Deuteronomy 6:4 from the Old Testament says:

"Hear, O Israel: The LORD our God is one LORD"

Pharisees, who were good in studying the scriptures and arguing by the meaning of each phrase and word, knew this verse very well and when Jesus claimed that He and the Father are one, they had conviction in their minds that Jesus was blaspheming God.

In John 10:17 Jesus brings out excellent truth that the Father loves Him, because He lays down His life that He might take it again.

It pleased the Father to bruise the Son, put him to grief when He shall make His soul an offering for sin. Jesus died for our sake; He was buried; yet Jesus was raised from the dead on the third day as it is written. (Isaiah 53:10)

"For he hath made him to be sin for us, who knew no sin; that we might be made the righteousness of God in him". (2 Corinthians 5:21)

"No man taketh it from me, but I lay it down of myself. I have power to lay it down, and I have power to take it again. This commandment have I

received of my Father" John 10:18

As Jesus was speaking about the Father and Himself that they are one, there was a division among Jews and one section of the Jews said that Jesus had devil in him while others argued that if he had devil in him, how would he heal the blind?

Jesus was walking in the temple in Solomon's porch on a feast day. It was the Feast of Dedication in winter when Jews surrounded him and asked him to say plainly if Jesus was the Christ. Jesus answered them and said that He told them already, yet they did not believe Him or His words or works that He did in His Father's name. Jesus said that the works of the Father that He did bear witness that He was the Son of God and He and the Father are one. His sheep hear His voice and they follow him, but they did not believe him or His works because they are not His sheep as He said before. That was the time when Jews took up stones to stone him to death, because they thought Jesus was blaspheming and blaspheme is punishable by stoning to death.

"Bring forth him that hath cursed without the camp; and let all that heard him lay their hands upon his head, and let all the congregation stone him. And thou shalt speak unto the children of Israel, saying, Whosoever curseth his God shall bear his sin. And he that blasphemeth the name

of the LORD, he shall surely be put to death, and all the congregation shall certainly stone him: as well the stranger, as he that is born in the land, when he blasphemeth the name of the LORD, shall be put to death". (Leviticus 24:14-16)

"And thou shalt stone him with stones, that he die; because he hath sought to thrust thee away from the LORD thy God, which brought thee out of the land of Egypt, from the house of bondage" (Deuteronomy 13:10). Compare also Deuteronomy 17:3-5, and 2 Samuel 12:14

This was not the first time Jews took up stones against Jesus to stone Him to death. John 8:51-59 show us that Jesus said that whoever keeps His words will not see death. Jesus was obviously affirming that those who believe in Him and keep His words will have eternal life, but Jews misunderstood him and said Abraham and prophets died and how that Jesus was saying that whoever keeps His words will not taste death.

Jesus said that their father Abraham rejoiced to see His day and saw it, and was glad (John 8:56). Jews, indeed, thought Jesus was speaking blasphemy because he was not yet fifty years old but he said before Abraham He was there. Jews took up stones to stone Him to death, but Jesus being divine walked away from their midst unharmed.

In John Chapter 10 also we see that they tried to stone Jesus in vain, and Jesus walked away from their midst unharmed. Jesus laid down His life when it was due time for Him to lay down His life. He laid down His life when it was appointed time for Him to lay down His life and took it back when it was due time.

The Body of Jesus did not see any corruption but was raised from the dead on the third day and He appeared to His disciples and many others who belonged to Him for forty days and then ascended into heaven. He is seated on the right hand of the Majesty and will come soon.

Jews said to Jesus that for they were not there to stone him for the good works He had been doing but for alleged blaspheme. That was the time when Jesus questioned them and shook their foundation of presuppositions. They thought Jesus was an ordinary man and that he was blaspheming God. They are aware of the books of Moses and more clearly Deuteronomy 6:4 according to which they, who were the children of Israel, were not supposed to have any other gods before Him. They knew that Jehovah is the true God and there is only one God, who is their LORD.

"Hear, O Israel: The LORD our God is one LORD"
Deuteronomy 6:4

In Exodus Chapter 20 the Ten Commandments

were given and the LORD said:

"*I am the LORD thy God, which have brought thee out of the land of Egypt, out of the house of bondage. Thou shalt have no other gods before me. Thou shalt not make unto thee any graven image, or any likeness of any thing that is in heaven above, or that is in the earth beneath, or that is in the water under the earth*" (Exodus 20:2-4)

That was a commandment that before the true God of Israel there shall be no other gods and they shall not worship any other god other that the LORD their God, who brought them out the land of Egypt redeeming them the bondage of slavery. In this context Jesus was saying that He was the Son of God, and He and the Father are one. Yet, his quotation from Psalm 82:6 was not to prove his coming to this world as "Messiah", or that Psalm 82:6 was a prophecy about Him.

The reason why Jesus quoted few verses from Psalm 82 was to thrash them on their own argument, and to shake the foundation of their presuppositions. Jesus did thrash their argument successfully and they walked away from them unharmed. To understand what Jesus was saying it is necessary that we should read Psalm 82 fully:

The Psalm said that God stands in the congregation of the mighty and judges among 'gods'. The Psalmist questions how long these 'gods' will judge unjustly and accept the persons of the wicked. The following verses are instructions to defend the poor and fatherless, do justice to the afflicted and needy, and deliver the poor and needy and help them to get rid out of the hand of the wicked.

The 'gods' are supposed to render justice but if they do not do justice they are answerable to God. Many 'gods' have gone their own way rendering injustice to many and they are all accountable to the LORD. They are 'gods' and they are all the children of the most High, yet they shall all die like men and fall like one of the princes. Then Psalmist invokes God in prayer to judge the earth because He inherits al nations.

The question is who those 'gods' about whom Psalmist wrote are and about whom Jesus quoted in John Chapter 10:34-36

Hebrew Strong's Number 430 is " 'elohiym" is transliterated as "el-o-heem'"

1. Definition: (plural)

a. rulers, judges

b. divine ones

c. angels

d. gods

2. (plural intensive - singular meaning)

a. god, goddess

b. godlike one

c. works or special possessions of God

d. the (true) God

e. God

In KJV it is occurs 2606 times. In Genesis alone it occurs 189 times. Some of the verses where this word occurs in different contexts are as follows:

"In the beginning God created the heaven and the earth". (Genesis 1:1)

"For God doth know that in the day ye eat thereof, then your eyes shall be opened, and ye shall be as gods, knowing good and evil". (Genesis 3:5)

"Then his master shall bring him unto the judges; he shall also bring him to the door, or unto the door post; and his master shall bore his ear through with an aul; and he shall serve him for ever" (Exodus 21:6)

"If the thief be not found, then the master of the house shall be brought unto the judges, to see whether he have put his hand unto his neighbour's goods". (Exodus 22:8)

"For all manner of trespass, whether it be for ox, for ass, for sheep, for raiment, or for any manner of lost thing, which another challengeth to be his, the cause of both parties shall come before the judges; and whom the judges shall condemn, he shall pay double unto his neighbour" (Exodus 22:9).

In all the above verses 'elo-heem' is God, whose name is Jehovah, or the judges of Israel who were representatives of God on this earth.

2 Chronicles 19:6 shows that the judges in Israel were delivering judgments as representatives of God. Not all the judges delivered justice but few delivered injustice also. It is about those judges, who rendered injustice that the Psalmist wrote about.

"And said to the judges, Take heed what ye do: for ye judge not for man, but for the LORD, who is with you in the judgment". (2 Chronicles 19:6)

In Genesis 3:5 Serpent said that if Eve ate the forbidden fruit Eve and Adam will be like 'gods'. It is misinterpretation that the serpent was suggesting to eat the fruit in order that she and Adam may become like other 'gods', the agents of Satan, but the suggestion was that they will be like God knowing good and evil.

The word 'elo-heem' is used in plural. God is

triune and this word was used to describe Him. When serpent said uttered this word to Eve, he was obviously saying to Eve that Adam and Eve (the two individuals) that they will be each like a God.

It does not suggest that Serpent was saying to Eve that Adam and Eve will be like judges or like evil gods or rulers. Interpretation that they would like judges or evil rulers is gross misrepresentation to undermine the meaning of the word of God.

At this juncture there are also two phrases brought in to misrepresent the 'elo-heem' in order to bring in confusion that the 'gods' referred to in Psalm 82 and John 10 are some mystical "gods", who ruled on earth.

The infusion of these two phrases is very appealing and interesting as if to project good knowledge of truth of Jesus.

The mystical figures are brought through assumptions to mislead the understanding of the deity of Lord Jesus Christ.

The two phrases are: "HOST OF HEAVEN" and the "LORD of hosts". They come from some oblivion into the thoughts of those who want to undermine the deity of Lord Jesus Christ.

It should be understood that Jesus was not

justifying in John 10:34-36 that Psalmist spoke of "Messiah" who was to come, but he was referring to earthly judges who rendered injustice and will face consequences of their deeds. Jesus was pointing to Jews, the learned men, who alleged Him that He spoke blaspheme.

Jesus quoted Psalm 82 to show that in the law that they knew of, it was written that

"Ye are gods, and all of you are the children of the most High" and the verse is followed by the next verse which says:

"But ye shall die like men, and fall like one of the princes"

Those are all judges in Israel who were the children of the most High appointed to render justice but failed in their duties as the children of the most High and the consequence is that they fall like one of the princes. They are not rulers over nations.

The phrase "HOST OF HEAVEN" is not used to represent evil gods or mystical figures, but they are stars and planets.

"Host" comes from Hebrew Strong's number 6635 which is transliterated as "Tsaba' ".

1. The definition is: that which goes forth, army,

war, warfare, host

a. army, host

1. host (of organised army)

2. host (of angels)

3. of sun, moon, and stars

4. of whole creation

b. war, warfare, service, go out to war

c. service

"Heaven" comes from Hebrew Strong's number 8064 "Shamayim".

1. The definition is: heaven, heavens, sky

a. visible heavens, sky

1. as abode of the stars

2. as the visible universe, the sky, atmosphere, etc

b. Heaven (as the abode of God)

Stephen said:

Then God turned, and gave them up to worship the host of heaven; as it is written in the book of the prophets, O ye house of Israel, have ye offered to me slain beasts and sacrifices by the space of forty years in the wilderness?" (Acts 7:42)

The "host of heaven" mentioned in Acts 7:42

refers to stars and heavenly bodies, about which is written in the book of prophets.

"Except the LORD of hosts had left unto us a very small remnant, we should have been as Sodom, and we should have been like unto Gomorrah". (Isaiah 1:9)

Amos also wrote about the planet Saturn. "But ye have borne the tabernacle of your Moloch and Chiun your images, the star of your god, which ye made to yourselves". (Amos 5:26)

There is no reason to bring in "HOST OF HEAVEN' AND OR "Lord of HOSTS" into proving that Jesus deity is strengthened based on Psalm 82. These are misrepresentations and misinterpretations.

Jesus caught Jews, who were ready to stone Him to death alleging that He blasphemed God, in their own argument and intelligence and thwarted their presuppositions.

Note the argument Jesus placed.

"If he called them 'gods', unto whom the word of God came"

"Say ye of him, whom the Father hath sanctified, and sent into the world, Thou blasphemest;"

"because I said, I am the Son of God?"

"If he called them gods, unto whom the word of God came, and the scripture cannot be broken; Say ye of him, whom the Father hath sanctified, and sent into the world, Thou blasphemest; because I said, I am the Son of God?" (John 10:35-36)

THE JUDGES AND THE JUDGMENTS

God gave the children of Israel several instructions besides Ten Commandments. These instructions are rather explanations and elaborations of each commandment. Anyone violating those instructions were judged and punished or provision for restitution is detailed.

Perusal of few instructions and the judgments will give us understanding as to who these judges (otherwise called 'elo-heem' in Hebrew language) were and how they were judged during Old Testament period.

If an Israelite buys a Hebrew servant the servant can be in his home as slave for only six years and in the seventh year he should be released.

However, if the slave finds it good to serve his master more than the period he was supposed to be under him the master shall bring the slave before the judge to the door, and his master shall pierce the ear of the slave by an awl unto the doorpost. Then shall the slave serve his master for ever (Exodus 21:1-8).

A thief stealing an ox or sheep kills the animal he should restore at the rate of five oxen for one ox killed and four sheep for a sheep.

If the thief is caught and he is killed there shall be no blood shed for him; but if it is during day time the thief shall be caught and delivered for judgment and restitution should be made to the one from whom the thief stole. If the restitution cannot be made the thief shall be sold as slave. If the thief caught in action is killed during day time it shall be treated as murder. (Exodus 22:1-8)

If a man entices a maid, who was not betrothed yet, and lie with her, he shall surely endow her to be his wife, but if the father of the maid refuses to give the maid to him, he shall pay money according to the dowry of virgins. (Exodus 22:16-17)

The three examples shown above are only to give an idea how the justice system worked during Old Testament period and how the judges rendered justice or injustice.

This is what is spoken of by the psalmist in Psalm 82. It was a Psalm of Asaph. He wrote that God who is the judge of all judges among the 'gods', that is the judges on this earth among the children of Israel.

Let us remember these commandments and instructions were given to the children of Israel and not to Gentiles.

There is, therefore, no scope of application of these commandments or instructions to Gentiles and the scriptures are not speaking of some mystical figures or some strange gods, or idols, but the judges mentioned here are simply the judges whom the scriptures call as 'gods' among the children of Israel.

Psalmist wrote about the judges who rendered injustice and became accountable to God, who is the judge of all. Psalmist calls for justice and invokes God's presence through his prayer that He may judge those judges ('gods'), who rendered injustice.

Jesus quotes those scriptures in John 10:34-36 and said that if scriptures, which cannot be broken, call these human judges in Israel as 'gods' to whom the word of God came, what is wrong if He calls himself, who is sanctified and sent into the world, as the 'Son of God', and why would it be tantamount to blaspheming?

Jesus was not trying to establish his deity here nor was saying that Psalm 82 was a prophecy about him. He quoted these verses from Psalm 82 just as a rabbinical argument to win over the so-called intelligent Pharisees who were trying to trap him and stone him to death.

Jesus thwarted their intelligence in their own conceit and won the argument. He walked away unharmed in spite of their approach to stone him to death. No one could do any harm to Jesus before His appointed time. He offered himself when it was appointed time for him to lay His life and He took his life back when it was due time.

CHAPTER 2
TRUTH

Satan is spiritually wicked and needs to be defeated by spiritually born again believer by wearing all the pieces of protective gear, never missing even one of them. Missing even one of them will endanger them to be defeated by Satan. Unless a believer takes refuge in Lord Jesus Christ as his helper he cannot be triumphant over wily and subtle efforts Satan to sabotage believer's life in Christ. It is the truth that is girt around loins that helps to defeat Satan. It is the belt of truth that holds fast few other weapons such as dagger and the sword when a soldier moves on his mission.

Lord Jesus Christ is the author of Truth and He is the Truth, and when a believer trusts Him as rock of refuge, He helps him to be truthful and defeats Satan, who is the father of lies.

Jesus saith unto him, I am the way, the truth, and the life: no man cometh unto the Father, but by me. (John 14:6)

Jesus said to Scribes and Pharisees that he was the light of the world and whoever followed him had the light of life and will not walk in darkness.

The Pharisees therefore accused him of his birth. When Jesus said to them that He was not alone but he and the Father were one, they did not understand him. They even asked him where his father was. Jesus told them that the record he bore was true and they knew him not fully well. (John 8:14-15).

Jesus was born of the Virgin Mary. Luke 1:35 records... "And the angel answered and said unto her, The Holy Ghost shall come upon thee, and the power of the Highest shall overshadow thee: therefore also that holy thing which shall be born of thee shall be called the Son of God". Jesus is the Son of God.

Jesus said to them that if they knew God they would have known him as well. The argument went on and Pharisees called names and said that he was Samaritan and he had a devil in him. Jesus said that he had no devil in him and they dishonored him but he honored his Father. (John 8:48-50) They did not believe him even though he spoke the Truth.

It can be seen that Jesus was very bold and point blank to give replies to them. Jesus tells them that they need to be freed of their sin. Scribes and Pharisees boasted in themselves that they are the children of Abraham and they were never under bondage that they should be freed from their sin.

They did not remember or were ignorant that their forefathers were in bondage of slavery under Pharaoh in Egypt; they did not remember or were ignorant that they were under the bondage of Assyrians and Babylonians.

At that point of time when they were talking to Jesus and as they were trying to trap Jesus on some question and they were already under the bondage of Roman Government. Yet, Jesus was making a point that they were under the bondage of sin and they need to be freed of their sin. Scribes and Pharisees did not realize that Jesus was the Messiah and he was the Son of God.

They were claiming that God is their Father and Jesus had to tell them bluntly that their father was devil because they could not recognize the Son of God nor could understand his speech. He said their father, who is the devil, was a murderer from the beginning and lived not in the truth because there is no truth in him. (John 8:41-44)

Jesus spoke the truth because He is the Way, He is the Truth and He is the Light. The Pharisees and Scribes lost their patience and were about to harm Jesus. Even as Jesus was speaking these words many believed; yet Scribes and Pharisees went on accusing him and tried to lay hands on him. The time was net yet come, and therefore, no one could do anything to Jesus and he walked away from their midst unharmed.

FALSE PROPHETS

"For I know the thoughts that I think toward you, saith the LORD, thoughts of peace, and not of evil, to give you an expected end" (Jeremiah 29:11)

Speaking to His children, through Jeremiah the prophet, God says that He knows the thoughts that He think towards them and they are of peace, and not of evil to give them an expected end. This verse is taken from a letter from Jeremiah, written at the behest of the Almighty God, to the residue of elders, priests, prophets who were surviving captivity in Babylon.

The letter reads that God, who is the LORD of hosts and also the God of Israel has caused the Jews to be carried captive from Jerusalem to Babylon. God asks them to build for themselves houses, live therein, plant gardens and ear fruit from the trees.

The instructions from God were that they should settle down in Babylon until the Almighty God Himself redeems them from their bondage. Their stay in Babylon was not pleasant as they were captives. They had lost their freedom, blessings and abundance in Zion where they lived under the care of Almighty God. Psalm 137 shows their plight under kind Nebuchadnezzar.

The psalm describes how they longed to be in Zion. They sat down by the rivers of Babylon, yea, they wept when they remembered Zion. They were asked by those who carried them captive that they may sing for them a joyful song. They insisted that they should sing a song of Zion. Then they complain and say how they would sing a song for them while they were in captivity.

The singer asks as to how he could sing LORD's song in a strange land; and then goes to add condition on himself that if he forgot Jerusalem his right hand may forger her cunning; and if he preferred not Jerusalem above his chief joy his tongue may cleave to the roof of his mouth.

As they were reeling under these pathetic conditions few false prophets were there to comfort them that their captivity would not be for a long time; but ends soon. They gave them false promises that their return to Jerusalem was imminent. This false promise was against what God wanted to do in their lives.

God had some other plans for them; that they should build houses in strange land, settle down there, and live happily until their redemption from Captivity. This redemption was to come forth by God Himself. Prophet Jeremiah's letter written under the authority of the LORD has clearly in it, the intentions of God.

Unless seventy weeks are completed as prophesied in Daniel 9th Chapter their captivity would not end. They remain there until God Himself redeems them. Then, there was no point in being sad in the days of their life in Babylon. But the false prophets were spreading false promises that their stay as captives will not be for long; but soon would it end and they return to Jerusalem, which is their land.

Jeremiah goes further to say that they may marry, beget sons and daughters and get their sons and daughters also married in order that they may also bear sons and daughters that they marry increase in population rather than diminishing.

Notice here, that Jeremiah never wrote that their sons could marry males and daughters could marry women, but the verse clearly defines the marriage rules; "take wives for your sons, and give your daughters to husbands, that they may bear sons and daughters".

The LORD was encouraging the children of Israel taken captive to increase in population through their marriages and lead a happy life there in captivity until the Lord returns. The LORD was not saying that they should cry the entire time they spend in captivity; but to be happy as long as they live there in captivity while God Himself provides their needs until He returns and redeems them.

Jeremiah's letter says that they should seek peace of the city where the Lord had caused them to be carried as captives and pray to the LORD for the city in order that they may have peace. He warns them that the LORD of hosts, who is the God of Israel, says that their false prophets and diviners may not get them into false hopes that their captivity would end soon. He says that those false prophets were not sent by the LORD.

The Lord says to them through Jeremiah's letter that after they have spent seventy years in Babylon He will visit them and perform His good word toward them in causing them to return to Jerusalem. He says that He knows the thoughts that He has toward the children of Israel; the thoughts of peace and not of evil, and that those thoughts will work towards the expected end; that is to bring it to pass the destiny that the LORD had designed for them.

The LORD knows what He does and what the children of Israel had to do in the meanwhile. They will be caused by the LORD to cry and pray unto Him for redemption. They will seek the LORD with all their heart. The LORD will hear them and they will find Him. They will receive answers to their prayers when they search for him with all their heart.

The LORD assures that He will be found when

they call upon Him and He will turn away their captivity. He will gather them from all the nations and from all the places. God had driven them to many places around the world; yet He will find them and bring them from those cities and nations into which He had caused them to be carried away captive.

For my people have committed two evils; they have forsaken me the fountain of living waters, and hewed them out cisterns, broken cisterns, that can hold no water. (Jeremiah 2:13)

"Cistern" is a container used for storing water or any other liquid. God says that those who put confidence in earthly objects are like holding water in broken cisterns. That is to say that water that is held in the cistern flows away and the end is disappointment and misery. But for those who take refuge in God will have blessings and God holds them intact. Before God punishes sinners he pleads with them to repent. He pleads so as to see that sinners plead with themselves.

God's love and His grace are like fountain that refreshes us, cleanses us. It is the living water for us. His love sustains us and supports us to maintain spiritual life. It is evil to forsake this life-giving fountain. People who take refuge in earthly objects are like those who make for themselves broken cisterns that cannot hold water.

God deals with each individual in a different way. He knows the best for each individual. He causes the individual to pray when it is time for Him to do some good for the individual. He knows best for each individual. God's thoughts reconcile with His actions.

Our works may not be according to our thoughts, but God's works always are in accordance with the thoughts that he had beforehand. Man may not have clear directions as to where his thoughts are heading to and resultant actions may not be the product of his thoughts. But in the case of God, it is not so. God has clear vision of what should come to pass in the lives of his children.

God does not repent for his actions.

And also the Strength of Israel will not lie nor repent: for he is not a man, that he should repent. (1 Samuel 15:29)

For I am the LORD, I change not; therefore ye sons of Jacob are not consumed. (Malachi 3:6)

His resultant actions are clear ending of the thoughts that he had for them.

Act 15:18 Known unto God are all his works from the beginning of the world.

Then shall ye call upon me, and ye shall go and

pray unto me, and I will hearken unto you. And ye shall seek me, and find me, when ye shall search for me with all your heart. (Jeremiah 29:12-13)

For I know the thoughts that I think toward you, saith the LORD, they are thoughts of peace, and not of evil, to give you an expected end (Jeremiah 29:11).

His thoughts are higher than ours.

For as the heavens are higher than the earth, so are my ways higher than your ways, and my thoughts than your thoughts. (Isaiah 55:9)

God thinks of bringing good end in the lives of His children. If it is paraphrased it could be like "if you follow your own thoughts you would end up in disaster...you do not think as you should...your thoughts are not clear...they are not leading to good end; the end of the road of your thoughts is destruction; disastrous... Take heed of me and my thoughts my thoughts are perfect towards you. I am not thinking of immediate advantages for you for my aim to see that your end does not end in disaster or destruction... Follow me.

CHAPTER 3. RIGHTEOUNESS

The child of God needs to be righteous and pure in order that he may defeat Satan, who is impure and father of temptations. Satan brings impurities and makes a believer impure when he falls into temptations of Satan even though God provides a way out from the temptations.

There hath no temptation taken you but such as is common to man: but God is faithful, who will not suffer you to be tempted above that ye are able; but will with the temptation also make a way to escape, that ye may be able to bear it. (1 Corinthians 10:13)

In Acts 7th Chapter we read Stephen, who had great faith and did miracles, explained the plight of Joseph before he was elevated as the great ruler. Before Joseph was sold into Egypt, Judah, one of the brothers of Joseph suggested that Joseph should not be put to death as his other brothers planned, but he be sold to Egyptians and make money out of the deal. All other brothers of Joseph agreed to Judah's plan and sold Joseph to Egyptians. They cast him in to a pit so that he may die but later pulled him out of the pit and sold him to Ishmeelites.

Joseph was brought down to Egypt and Potiphar, an officer of Pharaoh bought him from Ishmaeelites. Potiphar's wife had a bad eye for Joseph, who was good looking and fairly built. When she failed to seduce him into adultery she charged Joseph that he tried to molest her and Joseph was put in prison. (Genesis 39:1)

It was a long journey of troubles and trials for Joseph from his place in pit to Potiphar's home, and then to prison on false charges, and then from prison to the very high position in Egypt.

In all these circumstances God was with Joseph and He had a purpose for Joseph. God sent Joseph ahead of his father, mother, and his brothers to provide their needs during famine.

"But that on the good ground are they, which in an honest and good heart, having heard the word, keep it, and bring forth fruit with patience". (Luke 8:15)

DEAD IN TRESPASSES

Bible says we were dead in trespasses and sins; but to those who believed in Jesus Christ as personal savior, it is the quickening of the spirit. We, who are born again, are redeemed from the bondage of sin. We are saved unto eternal life.

Sin held us as slaves; made us blind to the truth of the Gospel of Jesus Christ; made us liable for condemnation; had us as aliens from the commonwealth of Israel; strangers to the covenants of promise; had us in a state of hopelessness, and it treated us a strangers and foreigners to the living God. But God delivered us and made us servants of righteousness.

We, who were the children of wrath are given the privilege of calling the living God, as 'Abba, Father'. He has given us the privilege of be called as sons of God. He has translated into the Kingdom of His dear Son.

Dead in trespasses does not mean that a man is fully dead in all respects to the extent that he cannot believe on Jesus, but it means that Satan has blinded his belief and understanding to the extent that the Scriptural truth appears to him as foolishness. (Ref: Ephesians 2nd Chapter, 2 Cor. 4:3-4, Romans 6:17-18, John 3:19-20, Mark 2:17, Luke 15th Chapter, Col 1:13)

The only demand that God has placed on a sinner is to repent of his sins and call on Jesus to forgive his/her sins. Entire price for redemption from sinful life is paid for by Jesus on the cross. There is nothing that a sinner needs to do except believing in the blood of Jesus, who paid the price for our redemption already.

God formed our bodies with the dust of the ground. When he created the first man, on this earth he breathed his life into the nostrils of the man and the man (Adam) became a living soul. The living soul that God created was in the image of God.

After man had committed sin he lost that image of God, and 'death reigned from Adam to Moses even over that had not sinned after the similitude of Adam's transgression'.

By the offence of one many came under the penalty of death, but by the gift of God that is 'grace' many have become eligible to receive eternal life. It was by one, (Adam), who sinned that death came to reign on man, and it is by the ONE (Jesus), that the gift of God is available for all sinners.

All those who accept that the Son of God, Jesus, died for his/her sins, and accept him as the 'Lord' of one's life are saved from damnation. It is then that the soul dead in trespasses is redeemed; it is then that the soul is delivered from suffering the wrath of God. The soul that does not repent of his/her sins will be cast into lake of fire, by God, after the 'Great white throne judgment', which is the final judgment.

As and when our earthly house of this tabernacle gets dissolved we gain a building of God, the house not made with hands, but that which would be eternal in heavens. We groan in this body desiring to be clothed upon with the house that we would have in heavens, and that glorified body, which resurrects from the dead, when Jesus comes again, would not be naked; but the living soul with eternal life that does not marry nor is given in marriage. (Ref: 2 Corinthians 5th Chapter Matthew 22:30 and Romans 5th Chapter)

Apostle Peter reveals a marvelous truth in 1 Peter 1st Chapter. Addressing to the strangers scattered throughout Pontus, Galatia, Cappadocia, Asia and Bithynia he calls on Elect by God the Father, and wishes them 'Grace'. All those, whom he addressed were, as he says, were begotten unto lively hope by the resurrection of Jesus Christ from the dead and to inherit incorruptible, and undefiled rewards that do not fade away. These are reserved for them in heaven.

If we read 2 Timothy 3:16 it says, *'All scripture is given by inspiration of God, and is profitable for doctrine, for reproof, for correction, for instruction in righteousness'.*

Depending upon 2 Timothy 3:16 every one, irrespective of his belonging to the clan of Jews or Gentiles can claim this verse to be applicable in one's life, provided he/she has accepted Jesus Christ as his/her personal Savior.

The power of God keeps us and assures us that inheritance, which is in heaven. We have the eternal life to be with the Lord Jesus Christ always. That inheritance is incorruptible, and undefiled. It does not fade away. We may face trials and tribulations in this world, but the rewards that are reserved for us in eternity are great and beyond description.

If we call on the Father, He will help us to pass our pilgrimage on this earth in fear of Him, rendering to Him His due worship. We are not redeemed by silver or gold, but by the blood of His only begotten Son Jesus Christ, whom John identified as the Lamb of God. Peter confirms that this Lamb of God was Lord Jesus. John said this is the Lamb of God came to this world to take away the sin of the world.

The Father in heaven judges every man according to his/her works while sojourning on this earth. He keeps record of our vain conversations that we may have received from our earthly fathers following traditions.

Therefore, let us keep in mind that as the Scripture says, Lord Jesus Christ was 'foreordained before the foundation of the world' and he was revealed unto us in the form of man. He died on the cross, bearing our sins, so that we may have redemption from sin. God raised him from the dead on the third day after crucifixion. Jesus is not dead lying in the grave just as any other man; but he was raised from the dead on the third day as prophesied.

Later, after forty days on this earth he ascended into heaven. He is now seated on the right hand of the Majesty, pleading on our behalf with the Father. Our faith in God increases as our days pass on this earth because of this infallible truth.

Our souls are purified by believing on this truth and hope increases as our sojourning on this earth tapers to start afresh eternal life with the only one, who paid the price for our salvation. Likewise, our love for one another should be fervent and pure. Just as grass withers, and flower fades, our life on this earth is also temporal and temporary, but the life with Jesus is eternal as the Word of God endures forever. (I Peter 1st Chapter)

Apostle Paul warned (in Romans 1st Chapter) all those Romans that they had changed the glory of the un-corruptible God into images of God's creation. They made beasts and creeping things and made them as their own gods. Therefore, 'God also gave them up to uncleanness through the lusts of their own hearts to dishonor their own bodies between themselves'.

But for those, who honor Lord Jesus Christ and

take refuge in him, there is hope that they will rise from the dead unto incorruption. The body of the believer in Christ is raised in power, even though on this earth he/she was in weakness. The believer in Christ rises in an incorruptible body that has natural body and also spiritual body. The first man Adam was made a living soul and the last Adam (Jesus) was made a quickening spirit. 1 Corinthians 15:42-45

It is a great blessing because we, who were dead in trespasses and sins, are also made quickened. Ephesians 2:1 And you hath he quickened, who were dead in trespasses and sins.

THE GOSPEL OF PEACE

Every true Christian will acknowledge that the word became flesh and dwelt among men and if any one does not recognize this fact surely he is not the servant of God, but false prophet or false teacher. The soldier will have good shoes to stand on and move on. Frail foot wear will drag him backwards. When the believer is shod with good shoe his tranquility is immense.

Hereby know ye the Spirit of God: Every spirit that confesseth that Jesus Christ is come in the flesh is of God: (1 John 4:2)

Now the Spirit speaketh expressly, that in the latter times some shall depart from the faith, giving heed to seducing spirits, and doctrines of devils; Speaking lies in hypocrisy; having their conscience seared with a hot iron; (1 Timothy 4:1-2)

"But God commendeth his love toward us, in that, while we were yet sinners, Christ died for us". (Romans Ch. 5:8)

While we were enemies to God Christ died for our sake. He loved us and had compassion on us. God is not human to take back the gift that He gives to believer in him. It is by hearing the Word of God that the sinner confesses his sins and trusts in the Lord. He lays his faith in God through Jesus Christ. It is the Father in heaven, who draws unto himself, those that are to be saved. Such faith comes by hearing the Word of God. He who receives Jesus as his personal savior is secure in God's arms. Holy Spirit leads the believer every day and guides *his paths.*

Ephesians Chapter 2:8-10 show us that this gift of salvation cannot be gained through any amount of works of man. No man can boast that he received salvation by doing good works but good works follow after a man has received salvation. We are the workmanship of God. Any sin is abominable to God and no sin will go unpaid for while the believer is on this earth.

PEACE FROM THE SON OF GOD

Jesus Christ is the Son of God and very God Himself. Jesus said, in John 10:30 "I and my Father are one".

He said in John 16:15 "All things that the Father hath are mine: therefore said I, that he shall take of mine, and shall show it unto you".

He said in John 17:11 "And now I am no more in the world, but these are in the world, and I come to thee. Holy Father, keep through thane own name those whom thou hast given me, that they may be one, as we are".

Apostle Paul wrote about Jesus Christ in Colossians 1:15-18 "Who is the image of the invisible God, the firstborn of every creature: For by him were all things created, that are in heaven, and that are in earth, visible and invisible, whether they be thrones, or dominions, or principalities, or powers: all things were created by him, and for him: And he is before all things, and by him all things consist. And he is the head of the body, the church: who is the beginning, the firstborn from the dead; that in all things he might have the preeminence".

The writer of Hebrews wrote about Jesus Christ, as follows:

Who being the brightness of his glory, and the express image of his person, and upholding all things by the word of his power, when he had by himself purged our sins, sat down on the right hand of the Majesty on high; (Hebrews 1:3)

John testified that Jesus was the Lamb of God. The next day John saw Jesus coming toward him and said, "Look, the Lamb of God, who takes away the sin of the world!" John 1:29

The verse in John Chapter 1 as cited above is the clear definition of who Jesus is. Jesus was the Word, He was with God and He is God Himself. Jesus is the creator of this world, he is the second person in the Trinity, consisting of God the Father, the Son and the Holy Spirit. God exists in three persons and God is One. The three are not three Gods but One God and three persons in One. They have different functions yet, they are One, co-equivalent, co-existent.

When Adam fell from the presence of God by sinning against God, he was sent out of Garden of Eden. The sin Adam committed by eating the forbidden fruit in the Garden of Eden is inherited by all of us. Jesus Christ, who is also called, the last Adam had to incarnate and come down from heaven to bear our sins and die in our stead.

"For God so loved the world that he gave his only begotten Son, that whosoever believeth in him should not perish, but have everlasting life". John 3:16

God loved us so much that He sent His one only one son Jesus Christ to this world for the remission of our sins. He was born of the virgin Mary, as a result of the works of the Holy Spirit and was raised a carpenter's house of His earthly parents Joseph and Mary. Jesus is the Son of God and God Himself.

Jesus said He is in the Father and Father in Him. Jesus is divine and human. While he was on this earth he had two natures one of divine and another of human. He did miracles and healed sick, and preached the Kingdom of God.

"All things are delivered unto me of my Father: and no man knoweth the Son, but the Father; neither knoweth any man the Father, save the Son, and he to whomsoever the Son will reveal him". Matthew 11:27

By offering Himself upon the cross of Calvary, Jesus opened the way for everyone to be saved. Jesus died for our sake as an atonement of sacrifice. Jesus, who is righteous, declares us righteous upon our confession of our sins.

"Whom God hath set forth to be a propitiation through faith in his blood, to declare his righteousness for the remission of sins that are

past, through the forbearance of God". Romans 3:25

Several sick were healed; the sins of several were forgiven by him, yet he was not accepted by the authorities at that time and was crucified. Romans chose Barabbas, a criminal to be released in place of him, and, therefore, the governor Pilate released Barabbas and handed over Jesus to be crucified.

"Jesus answered and said unto him, Verily, verily, I say unto thee, Except a man be born again, he cannot see the kingdom of God". John 3:3

They parted his garments, they scourged him, they hurled insults on him and crucified along with two thieves; yet Jesus was so kind on those who crucified them.

"Then said Jesus, Father, forgive them; for they know not what they do. And they parted his raiment, and cast lots". Luke 23:34

Jesus also forgave one of the thieves who was crucified along with him, when the thief made prayer to him to remember him when Jesus comes into His Kingdom. Jesus immediately to him,

"And Jesus said unto him, Verily I say unto thee, To day shalt thou be with me in paradise". Luke

23:43

But on the third day Jesus rose from the dead and after providing purification for our sins ascended to heaven and is seated at the right of the Majesty.

Jesus died upon the cross of Calvary so that we may be reconciled unto Him. There is no difference, whether we are Jews or Gentiles; He died for all of us, and rose from the dead and ascended in to heaven. We, who were His enemies, are made His children. The opposition that was caused between Heaven and Earth by our committing sins is removed once and for all, by the appeasement of our sins by Jesus Christ dying on the cross for our sake. We are reconciled unto God through His blood that was shed upon the cross of Calvary.

CHAPTER 4
FORGIVENESS FROM SON OF MAN

THE SON OF MAN

God incarnated and came into this world as the "Son of Man" and lived among us. He was the Son of God and the image of the Father Himself.

"Giving thanks unto the Father, which hath made us meet to be partakers of the inheritance of the saints in light: Who hath delivered us from the power of darkness, and hath translated us into the kingdom of his dear Son: In whom we have redemption through his blood, even the forgiveness of sins: Who is the image of the invisible God, the firstborn of every creature: For by him were all things created, that are in heaven, and that are in earth, visible and invisible, whether they be thrones, or dominions, or principalities, or powers: all things were created by him, and for him: And he is before all things, and by him all things consist. And he is the head of the body, the church: who is the beginning, the firstborn from the dead; that in all things he might have the preeminence".   (Colossians 1:12-18)

THE POWER TO FORGIVE SINS

But that ye may know that the Son of man hath power upon earth to forgive sins, (he said unto the sick of the palsy,) I say unto thee, Arise, and take up thy couch, and go into thine house. (Luke 5:24)

On a certain day when it appeared as a hay day for Pharisees, who were learned Jews, and doctors of law, came by from Galilee, Judea and Jerusalem and were in the house, where Jesus was teaching. Their motto was always to trap Jesus on some tricky question.

It was then that there came few men along with a man who was suffering from palsy for healing. Inasmuch as there was hardly any space in the home, which was filled with multitude of people, the men went onto the top of the house and let him down through a large space that was made by removing tiles. The man, who was suffering from palsy and lying in a bed on a couch, was then brought down into the midst in front of Jesus.

There are three facts seen in the healing of the man who was suffering from palsy.

1.   Was the sickness there in him for the glory of God, or was it because he was sinner?

Sickness need not be in a man because of his sin, but it may also be there in a man for the glory of God. Once, when the disciples of Jesus asked him, was it the blind man's parents or his sin that was the reason for his blindness, "Jesus answered, neither hath this man sinned, nor his parents: but that the works of God should be made manifest in him". (John 9:3). Likewise, the sickness and the death of Lazarus were also for the manifestation of the glory of Jesus (John 11:4).

In this case, where the palsy was placed before Jesus for healing it was not so. The palsy was sick because of his sin.

"And when he saw their faith, he said unto him, Man, thy sins are forgiven thee". (Luke 5:20)

Pharisees and teachers of the law began to reason as to how Jesus could forgive sins, because according to their worldly knowledge only God can forgive sins. They blamed that Jesus was speaking blasphemy.

2. Was Jesus divine and did he have power to forgive sins.

Jesus was fully human on this earth; yet he was divine. Jesus perceived their thoughts and asked them whether it was easier to forgive sins, or to heal the sick. Jesus asserted that he was the Son of God, and had the power not only to forgive sins, but also heal the sick. Then, Jesus said

"But that ye may know that the Son of man hath power upon earth to forgive sins, (he said unto the sick of the palsy,) I say unto thee, Arise, and take up thy couch, and go into thine house" (Luke 5:24)

The man who was sick of the palsy immediately rose before them, took up his bed and departed glorifying God, and they were all amazed.

3.   Is it possible for men to heal miraculously?

Thirdly, the miracles of healing, whether it be for the manifestation of glory of God, or for forgiving a sinner can be done by only God and none else. The forgiveness is received by sinner when he asks Jesus to forgive his sin.

SALVATION IS THE GIFT OF GOD

The gift of God is so precious that once it is given to a believer God cannot deny His own love toward us, nor can He deny His love toward His One and only Son, Jesus Christ that He takes back that gift from us.

The words of Lord Jesus Christ help us to understand that the salvation of a believer in Christ is secure and eternal. Jesus' own words as recorded in John 10:29 are beyond doubt that He holds us firm in his fold.

"My Father, which gave them me, is greater than all; and no man is able to pluck them out of my Father's hand". (John 10:29)

"Herein is love, not that we loved God, but that he loved us, and sent his Son to be the propitiation for our sins. (1 John 4:10)

Jesus also promised His disciples that whatever they ask of the Father in heaven in His name, He would give unto them. They did not belong to this world, and because they did not belong to the world, Jesus chose them. (John 15:16) Whoever receives Jesus as his/her personal Savior, to them God gave power to become the sons of God (John 1:12).

CHAPTER 5
SHIELD OF FAITH

Satan's greatest weapon is to shoot darts of doubts into the minds of believer. Christians need to have strong shield of faith and ever vigilant to encounter the darts of doubts that Satan constantly hurls at believer.

Satan's attempts toward damaging the faith of a believer are constant and never ceasing. It all started in the Garden of Eden when the serpent questioned Eve "hath God said..."   This question is still there and Satan uses this weapon always even against staunch believer in Christ.

Now the serpent was more subtil than any beast of the field which the LORD God had made. And he said unto the woman, Yea, hath God said, Ye shall not eat of every tree of the garden? (Genesis 3:1)

Undaunted of his life Peter stood for truth and He had great faith in Jesus Christ.   He was a man of power and grace from God, and he spoke elaborately outwitting the knowledge of the high priest. The elders, scribes and the people brought him to stand before high priest to face the false charges lodged against him.

Stephen defended by speaking about Abraham with whom God made covenant and explained in detail about the Almighty God, who dwelt not in the temples made with hands but whose throne is Heaven, and whose footstool is the earth. He spoke about the God of Israel who delivered the children of Israel from the bondage of slavery and he spoke about Moses whom God had appointed as the leader to stand boldly before Pharaoh. He spoke of about Joseph whom God had sent ahead of his parents and his brethren to Egypt to find sustenance for them before there came great famine in the land of Egypt and Canaan.

Stephen gave the God of Israel the glory due unto His name. He did not speak blasphemy but recognized the protection he gave to his children. He spoke of the mighty power of God that humbled all his enemies and the enemies of the children of Israel. He did not speak a word against Lord Jesus Christ; rather he gave glory unto name of Lord Jesus Christ. As the people stoned him he called upon Lord Jesus Christ and prayed to receive his spirit. And, even as he was breathing his last, he said, 'lay not this sin to their charge'.

"And they stoned Stephen, calling upon God, and saying, Lord Jesus, receive my spirit. And he kneeled down, and cried with a loud voice, Lord, lay not this sin to their charge. And when he had said this, he fell asleep". (Acts 7:59-60)

LAW AND GRACE

Apostle Paul admonishes Galatians in no uncertain terms for believing in works associated with salvation. The word he used is 'bewitched'. He was not only asking them as to who has cast a spell over their understanding or enchantment, or fascinated them about their belief that law would save them and works were associated with their salvation, but called them 'fools' (Galatians 3:1) for such belief as they hold that law and works could save them.

The word 'fools' used here does not demean them that they lack wisdom and prudence, but he demeans their misunderstanding that they must do something under the law to God in recompense to what he has done for us. The meaning of 'fool' here was similar to what Jesus meant in Matthew 7:26.

The whole chapter of Galatians 3 deals with this subject of law versus grace. He not only questions them if there is anyone in the world, who is perfect in flesh, but also provides answers to his questions that no one could be saved by the law and works associated with it. He goes on to say that only faith in Jesus Christ, who redeemed us from the curse of the law, could save us. Abraham believed God, and it was reckoned unto him as righteousness. He says that the children, who are of faith, are the children of Abraham.

The Scriptures foresaw that God would justify the heathen through faith, and made available to us, the Word, through preaching, and made available this preaching even before the proclamation of the gospel unto Abraham that in him shall all nations be blessed. Obviously, this indicates that those, who are of faith in Christ, are blessed with faithful Abraham.

Apostle goes on, further, saying that those, who, think that they are still under the works of the law, subject themselves to be under the curse, inasmuch as it written in the Scriptures that whoever continues to believe in becoming perfect by obedience to the commandments written in the law is cursed; no one can be justified before God under the law.

The just shall live by faith and it is certain that the law is not of faith, but whosoever, tries to believe that law would save them would live by them, and would be under the curse. Lord Jesus indeed came to save his own, but when they rejected him, salvation was made available for Gentiles. No doubt this was in the plan of God, and this mystery was revealed in Romans 11:6-11. He came into this world to provide a way out from these stringent laws, and provided a way for everyone, that by faith in him a person is saved by grace.

Jesus was hung on the cross and bore our sins so that we may not be cursed. It is written that 'cursed is everyone that hangeth on a tree'. He came into this world so that the blessing of Abraham would be available for Gentiles through him, so that the gentiles also may receive the promise of the Spirit through faith.

There seems to arise a question in the minds of those, who have no good understanding about law versus grace as to why then God gave law in the first place and then asked us to be under 'grace'.

Apostle Paul writes that the law is not against the promises of God, but it was given in order that man may understand that the transgressions he committed cannot be forgiven by law, which only points out the guilt of a person. Under the law priest had to offer sacrifice first and then offer a sacrifice for the person, who is guilty.

If law could make a person righteous the life truly righteousness should have been by law, but the Scripture has concluded all under sin. The promise by faith of Lord Jesus Christ was made available only to those who believe.

The law was our schoolmaster in order to teach us the way unto Jesus, who is the only mediator, and we can be justified only by faith in him. After Jesus had become propitiation for us, it is not required of us to do what is to be done under the law in order to have salvation; but faith in him alone is enough and that is to say that we are no longer under schoolmaster.

As many as have believed and accepted Jesus Christ as personal Savior and Lord, have put on Christ, irrespective of whether they are Jew or Greek, bonded or free, or male or female. All those, who are saved with the precious blood of Jesus Christ are one in him and we belong to him and we are Abraham's seed by faith and have inherited the promises.

Apostle Paul blesses those, who do not voluntarily subject themselves to be under the yoke of law, but accept Christ's death upon the cross. He says fulfilling the law of Christ is more important than that of the Old Testament laws.

No one should boast of himself nor glory himself/herself, but everyone should glorify Lord Jesus Christ, whose marks were borne by not only Apostle Paul but all those, who realize the efficacy of the blood of Lord Jesus Christ.

Paul feels as if he was under the travail of child birth to explain to Galatians the difference between law and grace, and how hard it is to be under law rather than accept 'grace' alone as the way for salvation. He calls them, now, 'my little children', and try to explain to them about the implications in believing that law and works only would save them.

Galatians were under the erroneous belief that law and works only can save them. They desired to take pride in a list of rules they prescribed for them and as they keep the rules they would consider them as perfect. That, in other words, renders a notion that man can earn his own salvation by keeping a set of rules, like being good and doing good etc.

These things help men to be good men but would not secure salvation that is available free of cost as a result of belief in the works of Jesus, the Son of God, did for men. He came down into this world to redeem us from the bondage of sin, and, therefore, took upon himself, our transgressions and died for our sake. The fruits of the Holy Spirit are love, joy, peace, longsuffering, gentleness, goodness, faith, Meekness, temperance.

A saved man will have in him the Spirit of God and will have the fruits of the Holy Spirit. However, possession of these good qualities without accepting Jesus as 'Lord' will not make us a man eligible to have eternal life. The only way to have eternal life is to believe in the efficacy of the blood of Jesus Christ and accept the fact that he died in our stead on the cross.

Paul explains to Galatians, just as a matured man explaining to children that all those who believe that law can save them are like those, who are of 'bondwoman' and all those who believe in the 'grace' of Jesus are like those, who are of free woman. He quotes from Old Testament the things that have happened in Abram's life as described in Genesis 16th Chapter.

Sarai sent her handmaid, Hagar to sleep with Abram, and a son was born. It was legalism on the part of Sarai and Abram a method that finds a way out for them. Later a son was born to Abraham and his wife Sarah as a consequence of the promise of God to them. This son of the promise of God was of faith in God and His grace.

The son, who was born to Hagar was of the flesh, and the son born of promise to Sarai, was blessed. The posterity of bondwoman are still under bondage of Mosaic law, and the posterity of the free woman, who are supposed to be free from the bondage of Mosaic law, have unfortunately, embraced the law and works as their way for salvation, rejected Messiah as their Savior, and are still under the bondage of law.

Paul allegorizes these two to 'Agar', which is in mount Sinai that answers to Jerusalem, which is on this earth. Paul desires that everyone should embrace the belief that it is by 'grace' of God that saves a man. Paul allegorizes this to the Jerusalem, which is above all, that consists of the posterity of Isaac, born of Sarah and that 'grace' alone saves a person.

The legalists still insist that it is right to be under the law and keep the law to be saved. Such legalism will lead to the belief that there is no justification by the grace of God, but their own works will lead them to have eternal life.

Speaking of law and grace and the firm belief of Jews in their belief of laws plus works for their salvation rather than depending on pure mercy of God by grace through faith, another point that could we could meditate is on the fact as to why God did not have his own people, Jews, realize this so quickly that pure grace from God is alone sufficient for their salvation.

There is enough reason, as we understand, that God not only wanted his own people, Jews, to have their salvation, but also Gentiles to enjoy that privilege of calling him as 'Abba, Father'..

Apostle Paul wonders if God cast away his people and immediately reaffirms that it was not so, because he was also of the seed of Abraham, of the tribe of Benjamin. God did not cast away his people, whom he foreknew. Even when Elias was taking pride in himself that he was alone available to intercede on behalf of Israel, God says to him, that he had reserved seven thousand men unto him, who could intercede on behalf of Israel.

If the salvation, therefore, is by 'grace', then it is not by 'works'. What then happened exactly that their attitude and belief has not changed yet? Yes, it is because God blinded their eyes and gave them spiritual slumber, that they should not see and that they may not have ears for hearing unto this day. Have Israel stumbled that they should fall then?

Apostle Paul himself answers these questions (Romans 11th Chapter) that God did not blind them or made them deaf because of they were stumbling blocks nor is it because they have stumbled, but because of the desire God had that everyone in the world, irrespective of Jews or Gentiles be saved and have eternal life.

This is the difference between the earthly Jerusalem and the new Jerusalem that comes down from heaven. John saw a new heaven and a new earth after the first heaven and the first earth passed away and there was no more sea.

In this New Jerusalem there was not seen any difference between Jews or Gentiles, but those who were there were all one in Christ. They had put on righteousness of Christ as their garments. They had received Jesus as their personal Savior and Lord by grace through faith in him.

More than anyone taking of airs of his belonging to any clan the important fact that is to be borne in mind is that it is the grace of God that saves a man. No man needs precious metals such as gold and silver to earn a place in new Jerusalem, but all that a man needs is to have simple faith in Jesus, the Son of God and make him Lord of his/her life. God wipes away their tears.

There shall be no more death, no more sorrow, and no more crying and no more pain. God shall give freely to all that thirst for such a life the fountain of life. He who overcomes the world and the temptations therein shall inherit the blessings from God and he shall be His son.

Apostle Paul explains elaborately the plan of God for the salvation of Gentiles in Romans 11th Chapter. It was not because Israel have stumbled nor because they were stumbling blocks to anybody that their eyes were blinded and their ears were short of hearing and understanding who their Messiah was and what exactly they needed to do for their salvation. They always insisted that because God had done something for them they owe to God something that they essentially do and such recompense only will fetch their salvation. It is because of their misunderstanding that salvation is come unto the

Gentiles.

Paul warns Gentiles that they are like grafted wild olive tree in the places, where the branches of the natural branches were broken off. The Gentiles are partakers of the root and fatness of the natural olive tree. Therefore, he says, Gentiles should not be of high-minded, but fear.

The branches of the natural olive tree were broken off by God himself, because of their unbelief, and the Gentiles, who were like wild olive trees have, now, the sap and blessings from the root of the natural olive tree.

If Gentiles were to be high-minded and take pride in themselves or their own merits, God will not hesitate to chastise them. If God did not spare the natural branches of the olive tree would he tolerate the grafted olive tree; never!

Apostle Paul emphasizes in Romans 6th chapter that sin shall not have dominion over a born-again child because he/she is not under the law, but under grace. Those who seek to do good works and earn salvation by their own works have nullified the importance of blood of Jesus Christ and in their lives the blood of Jesus Christ that cleanses the sin has no value for them. They diligently keep doing good works neglecting the repeated emphasis from the Lord Jesus Christ that his blood saves and gives eternal life to all those, who go to him and accept him as the Lord.

After having been delivered from the bondage of sin by grace through faith should a child of God keep sinning because he is under the grace but not under law? Paul very firmly says, "God forbid". Never should a child of God return to sin and lose blessings from God. Salvation is not lost for those who are saved in the blood of Jesus Christ\; however, the Scripture does not endorse repeated sinning. God will surely chide and chastise the one that falls repeatedly into sin and seeks grace time and again.

Should we not consider the fact that if he yield to sin we are servants to sin and sin becomes our master; we are under grace and we should remain servants to our Lord and be of obedience to righteousness.

We were, once, servants of sin, but after accepting Jesus as our master, we have become servants of righteousness. We have our fruit unto holiness, and everlasting life. The law has concluded all of us under sin, but the gift of God is eternal life through Lord Jesus Christ.

'Gospel' means good news. Gospel of Jesus Christ means good news of Jesus Christ. There is another gospel about which Apostle Paul writes in Galatians 1:6 'I marvel that ye are so soon removed from him that called you into the grace of Christ unto another gospel'. This 'another gospel' dispels the efficacy of the blood of Jesus Christ and gives importance to law and works associated with it.

Paul writes to the Church in Thessalonica that when they received the word of God that they heard from Paul. He also thanked that they did not received the gospel not as the word of men, but as truth from the word of God that works effectually works only in those who believe in it. (1 Thessalonians 2:13)

In 1 Corinthians 15th Chapter Paul speaks of Resurrection of Jesus Christ and our resurrection. This is good news for those who have hope in Jesus Christ and believe that he is the savior. This gospel will benefit only those who receive it and believe in it. If one does not believe in the gospel of Jesus Christ and about the resurrection a sinner, who repents of his sin and accepts Jesus as his/her personal savior, the gospel is of no use to him.

Paul writes that he delivered good news that which he first received and believed. He writes in 1 Corinthians 15th Chapter 3 to 4 verses that Christ died for our sins according to Scriptures; and that he was buried; and that he rose again the third day according to the Scriptures. This is the good news and there is no other way for salvation than to believe in Jesus as personal Savior and that his death upon the cross only was the way for our salvation. In his resurrection we have the great news that there is none who rose from the dead, the way the Lord Jesus was raised.

Jesus, the Son of God, is our peace; he has broken down the middle wall of partition between us and the Father. He has abolished in his flesh the enmity that had us captive under the law of commandments contained in ordinances. He has done this to make us new, and did this for our sake to help us have peace with the Father. He preached peace to us, who were far off and also to those who were near. Through Jesus we have now access by one Spirit unto the Father. This is the reason why we are longer strangers and foreigners, but we are now fellow-citizens with saints, and we are the members of His house.

Why then should we serve the law? The law was added because of transgressions until 'the seed should come to whom the promise was made. Jesus, having become the mediator did not become lower in stature nor in status, and he is not a mediator of one, but God is one.

There is one God, and the mediator between the Father and us is the man Christ Jesus, who received an excellent ministry of a better covenant that was established on better promises. He redeemed us from the transgressions of the first testament in order that we, who are called, 'might receive the promise of eternal inheritance'.

The blood of Jesus shed upon the cross speaks better things than that of Abel, who brought of the firstlings of his flock and its fat, which was pleasing to God.

The two commandments that Jesus gave to New Testament believers have in them the essence of all the Ten Commandments. The two commandments the Jesus gave are:

  'And thou shalt love the Lord thy God with all thy heart, and with all thy soul, and with all thy mind, and with all thy strength: this is the first commandment. And the second is like, namely this, Thou shalt love thy neighbour as thyself. There is none other commandment greater than these' Mark 12:30-31

(Ref: Gen 4:4, Galatians 3rd Ch. 1 Timothy 2:5, Hebrews 8, 9 and 10th Chapters)

When someone insists on keeping the law in order to obtain salvation and be counted as righteous before God, and tries to be perfect in all respects, it needs introspection if the person is indeed keeping all the provisions of the law given by God, for even in keeping the law meticulously the law finds him guilty on one count or the other.

The only recourse left for man is to take refuge in the 'grace' of God given abundantly to us, through His only begotten Son Jesus Christ. As written in Romans 2 Chapter, those without the law shall perish without law, and those that have sinned in the law will become liable for judgment under the law.

Inasmuch as the law was given by God through Moses, Gentiles are reckoned as having no law, and therefore, if they try to obey the law meticulously, they are making the law unto themselves; the law that was not given by God. They accuse and excuse one another according to their own law.

As for Jews the Scripture calls them 'blind' who guide the 'blind', a light of them who are in 'darkness', an instructor of the 'foolish', a teacher of 'babes', Scriptures asks Jews, who teach others about law, as to why they do not teach unto themselves the law and strict provision therein?

If they are true to their teaching, then are they not stealing, while teaching not to steal? Why do they commit adultery? Bible is very strict on them that they being teachers of the law, they break the law and commit idolatry, resulting in blasphemy of God among the Gentiles. Circumcision profits only if the law is kept in perfect sense, but if one of the provisions of the law is broken, circumcision is tantamount to un-circumcision.

The punishments under law are very severe. Neither Jew nor Gentile can have redemption from their sins, if they rely on keeping the law and be justified. God invites everyone to accept 'grace' available through Jesus Christ, the only begotten Son of God and receive salvation. (Romans 2:12-29)

CHAPTER 6
HELMET OF SALVATION

And take the helmet of salvation, and the sword of the Spirit, which is the word of God: (Ephesians 6:17)

A man's head holds vital parts. They include brain in the skull. Unless the brain is protected very well a man will surely die. Even if the brain is hurt in a very small way it brings in huge damage in the life of man.

It is quite often seen how man suffers brain injuries, concussions, and spinal cord injuries in accidents never to regain their previous happy life; rather they become useless or confined to wheel chair for ever until they die.

It is, therefore, very essential that we wear helmet of salvation that Lord Jesus gave to us free of cost when we believed in Him.

But let us, who are of the day, be sober, putting on the breastplate of faith and love; and for an helmet, the hope of salvation. (1 Thessalonians 5:8)

A well-established faith in our salvation and hope

of our salvation will retain us strong in the Lord during spiritual conflicts. Enemy might strike us with doubts of our salvation by pointing at our past sins, but a well-established faith in the Lord will help us rebut those strikes from the enemy

It is, therefore, very imperative that we live in Christ always. Salvation is never lost, but by not taking care of our spiritual life and falling into temptations we become unfruitful to the Lord, thus losing many blessings from Him.

Ye are bought with a price; be not ye the servants of men. (1 Corinthians 7:23)

OUR SALVATION IS SECURE

In spite of charging believers that they have false hope in security of salvation and that salvation can be lost if a believer sins in his day-to-day life, the reasoning about the efficacy of the sacrifice of the Son of God gives us enough faith beyond doubt that the believer's salvation is eternally secured.

The work of God rendered through His One and only begotten Son, Lord Jesus Christ in extending His grace toward us is everlasting one, which will not be taken back by Him on any reason.

We are sealed with the Holy Spirit unto redemption and the reasoning that salvation of a believer can be lost is untenable. An important fact that should be noted is that a true believer will not sin but will stand firm in his faith in the Lord. The Scriptures say that one that commits sin is of the devil and one that is born of God does not commit sin (1 John 3:8-9). These verses show us that one can have assurance that believer is secure eternally while at the same time one that constantly seeks refuge in the hope that the security of salvation is not a true believer, but is yet to come to the Lord in the true sense of the repentance and acceptance of Lord Jesus as one's own personal Savior.

THE LOVE OF GOD

"Who shall lay anything to the charge of God's elect? It is God that justifieth. Who is he that condemneth? It is Christ that died, yea rather, that is risen again, who is even at the right hand of God, who also maketh intercession for us. Who shall separate us from the love of Christ? shall tribulation, or distress, or persecution, or famine, or nakedness, or peril, or sword? As it is written, For thy sake we are killed all the day long; we are accounted as sheep for the slaughter. Nay, in all these things we are more than conquerors through him that loved us. For I am persuaded, that neither death, nor life, nor angels, nor principalities, nor powers, nor things present, nor things to come, Nor height, nor depth, nor any other creature, shall be able to separate us from the love of God, which is in Christ Jesus our Lord". (Romans 8:33-39)

Apostle Paul shows us the love of God in Romans 8:33-39 that none can separate us from the love of God inasmuch as the Son of God, Jesus Christ, our Lord died for us, rose from the dead, ascended into heaven and seated on the right hand of the Majesty.

The fact that our Lord Jesus is interceding on behalf of us with the Father in heaven without ceasing is another reason to believe that believer is secure and his salvation is secure lest it should mean that the intercession of the only begotten Son Jesus Christ on behalf of us is in vain and has no effect.

The Father in heaven cannot deny Lord Jesus Christ's intercession on behalf of us. The feign thoughts that God, the Father in heaven, can deny the intercession of His One and only begotten Son, Lord Jesus Christ are too presumptuous to be taken as true.

The salvation given to a believer as a merciful gift by His grace be taken back, by the One, who sent His Only begotten Son for our sake.

No doubt, the believer in Christ makes himself/herself accountable for the sins he/she commits in his/her life time on this earth, for the sins he/she commits and may lose his/her rewards from God at the 'Bema Seat of Christ', when they are judged for their works for Him. Salvation can neither be earned through the works of a man nor can it be purchased for a price.

It is the gift of God, through Lord Jesus Christ, who paid the price for our sins upon the cross of Calvary, where He shed His precious blood for our sake and washed us in His blood.   The love of God is so great that He found us in our trespasses and sent His One and Only Son, Jesus Christ for our sake, that whosoever shall believe in Him shall not perish but have everlasting life.

If we confess our sins, He is faithful and just to forgive us our sins. He sought us because He loved us first.

We received salvation not because we loved Him first, but because He loved us first. While we were yet in sins and enemies to God, He loved us and compassion on us.

God is not human that such gift from Him that He gave to us would be taken back by Him from the believer, who trusts in Him and receives Jesus as his/her personal savior.

It is by hearing the Word of God that the sinner confesses his/her sins and reposes faith in God through His Son, who died for him/her and becomes a believer in Christ.

It is the Father in heaven, who draws unto himself, those are to be saved. Such faith comes by hearing the Word of God, and he, who receives Jesus as his/her personal savior is secure in His arms. Holy Spirit leads the believer every day and guides his/her paths.

No temptation has ever over taken any believer that he could not find an alternative way to escape from such temptation.

God provides alternative so that the believer may not fall into sin. In spite of such provision available, if believer commits sins he/she will receive chastisement from God and not only suffers in this world, but also loses rewards in eternity, but not salvation because believer is sealed with the Holy Spirit.

It is the gift of God and a firm promise from God, who will not break His promises. Notwithstanding any doubt that arises in believer about his/her salvation, believer's salvation is secure and eternal.

God is trustworthy and faithful that once He gives eternal life to a believer He will keep His promises and gives the believer redemption of his soul from all sins.

The gift of God is not so feeble or frail that it can be taken by God, nor is Jesus Christ's intercession on behalf of the children of God is so feeble that the Father in heaven refuses His intercession. The Holy Spirit's works, guidance, conviction of the guilt of believer are not so weak that His work can be of no avail in this world before He ends His work on the second coming of Jesus.

The gift of God is so precious that once it is given to a believer God cannot deny His own love toward us, nor can He deny His love toward His One and only Son, Jesus Christ that He takes back that gift from us.

SALVATION IS THE GIFT OF GOD

Romans 6:23 is a very familiar verse in the Bible. There is one great gift that God gave unto us through His One and Only Son Jesus Christ and that gift is the salvation and it is the greatest gift of all.

Wages are the earnings for the work done by someone. Bible calls the wages of sin is death, but the gift of God is eternal life through Jesus Christ our Lord

The Father in heaven in His mercy sent His One and Only Son Jesus Christ because He loved us first, even when we were dead in our trespasses and saved us by grace.

The believer, who has truly tasted that love from God and received the gift of salvation, cannot think of falling into sin and be away from that grace leading him into repentance again and again that, which would mean crucifying Lord Jesus afresh repeatedly and putting Him to open shame.

Hebrews 6:4-6 reminds us of this fact that a believer, who is enlightened and tasted His heavenly gift, will not think of falling into sin every day to seek refuge under the provisions in the Scriptures about the security of the believer and security of the salvation, but would rather lead a holy life pleasing unto the Lord.

We are saved by the grace of God through faith and not of ourselves but it is the gift of God.

Ephesians 2:8-10 show us that this gift of salvation, which is so precious, cannot be gained through any amount of works of man that anybody could boast of such good works, but we are the workmanship of God. Man may rob one to pay another to earn laurels from the latter but God knows the inner thoughts of man.

Speaking to His disciples, Jesus said that He would no longer call them as 'servants', but would call them as friends inasmuch as servant would not know what his master does. The disciples had no choice of becoming His disciples, but it was Jesus, who chose them as His disciples and ordained that they should go and bring forth fruit unto the Lord.

Herein lies the greatest love that God showed unto us that He chose us and ordained us to be his children.

We love him because He loved us first (1 John 4:16). Jesus also promised His disciples that whatever they ask of the Father in heaven in His name, He would give unto them. They did not belong to this world, and because they did not belong to the world, Jesus chose them. (John 15:16)

Whoever receives Jesus as his/her personal Savior, to them God gave power to become the sons of God (John Jesus gives eternal life to all those, who believe in Him, so that they shall never perish, nor can anyone pluck the believer out of His hand.

The Word of God is so clear here in John 10:28-30 that no one can pluck a believer out of His hand.

"And I give unto them eternal life; and they shall never perish, neither shall any man pluck them out of my hand. My Father, which gave them me, is greater than all; and no man is able to pluck them out of my Father's hand. I and my Father are one". (John 10:28-30)

A believer can trust in the words of Lord Jesus Christ, just as Apostle Paul affirmed in Romans 8:38-39, that neither anyone or any act, or any power, can separate us from the love of God, because we are in Christ Jesus and let us, therefore, give thanks unto the Father in heaven, just as Apostle Paul asked us to do in Colossians 1:1-13, that God made us partakers in the inheritance of the saints in light and for delivering from the power of darkness in order to translate us into the Kingdom of His One and Only Son, Jesus Christ.

We believe in the gospel of Jesus Christ and about the eternal life that Jesus promised unto us and we are sealed with the Holy Spirit of promise.

We are purchased possession of our God so that we may be unto him the praise of his glory. We should bear in mind the hope of our calling, and know "what the riches of the glory of his inheritance in the saints" (Eph.1:13-18)

WHAT DOES HANDING OVER TO SATAN MEAN?

"Of whom is Hymenaeus and Alexander; whom I have delivered unto Satan, that they may learn not to blaspheme" (1 Timothy 1:20)

Writing to Timothy Apostle Paul instructs a very

severe castigation. Corinthian Church was wicked and in the church there was a man who had committed adultery with his step mother. This sin was intolerable in the sight of God and man.

Therefore, Paul writes that the man who did such heinous sin may be handed over to Satan to persecute his body and flesh with the sincere expectation that his soul shall be saved to be with the Lord for ever and ever.

"This charge I commit unto thee, son Timothy, according to the prophecies which went before on thee, that thou by them mightest war a good warfare; Holding faith, and a good conscience; which some having put away concerning faith have made shipwreck: Of whom is Hymenaeus and Alexander; whom I have delivered unto Satan, that they may learn not to blaspheme" (1 Timothy 1:18-20)

THE SEVERITY OF JUDGMENT

For if we sin wilfully after that we have received the knowledge of the truth, there remaineth no more sacrifice for sins, (Hebrews 10:26)

The writer of Hebrews warns about the severity of the judgment of God that falls on those that sin willfully trampling down the sacrifice of our Only High Priest, Lord Jesus Christ and apostatizes. Hebrews 10:26-31 deal with this dilemma that

Christians attribute to salvation being lost in case a believer in Christ commits sin. These verses show us the importance of realizing who the Son of God is, and the results deliberate denial and renunciation of the faith in Christ fetches.

In the Old Testament the greatest of all punishments was awarded to deliberate denial of the Word of the LORD. "Because he hath despised the word of the LORD, and hath broken his commandment, that soul shall utterly be cut off; his iniquity shall be upon him" (Numbers 15:31).

Such punishment as is mentioned in Numbers 15:31 is awarded to those, who deliberately renounce the Son of God and tread Him down under foot.

The recognition of the efficacy of the blood of Jesus Christ and his High Priest-hood stands out to be the dominant demand from anyone in the world. One that is saved will never renounce Lord Jesus Christ and the efficacy of His blood shed upon the cross of Calvary.

It is, therefore, beyond doubt that only unbeliever can tread down the Son of God under his feet and face the serious consequences of being thrown into the 'lake of fire'.

The believer in Christ is secure eternally inasmuch as his belief in Lord Jesus Christ as his personal savior involves inseparable union with Christ and the death to sin (Romans 6:6-8). If any believer in Christ strives to trample upon the Son of God and denies Him, God will make him kneel down on his feet with enough chastisement, and acknowledge that Jesus is the Lord, and reaffirm that He is the Savior.

THE FEAST OF ATONEMENT

"Also on the tenth day of this seventh month there shall be a day of atonement: it shall be an holy convocation unto you; and ye shall afflict your souls, and offer an offering made by fire unto the LORD". (Leviticus 23:27)

The feast of "Day of Atonement" was celebrated by Israelites on the tenth day of seventh month. This is the sixth feast of the seven feasts described in Leviticus Chapter 23.

The great day of atonement ("Atonement" is called as "propitiation" in the New Testament) was on the day when Jesus was crucified on the cross of Calvary bearing our sin in the outside the gates of the city. Gospel writers Matthew, Mark, and John used the word "Golgotha", which means "place of skulls".

Luke used the word "Calvary" instead of "Golgotha" and Calvary means "Cranium" which again means the same as "skull". (Matthew 27:33,

Mark 15:22, Luke 23:33, John 19:17)

The picture drawn as shadow in the Old Testament in the Book of Leviticus Chapters 16 and 23 are fulfilled in the crucifixion of Lord Jesus.

The feast of "Day of Atonement" is celebrated by Israelites as a memorial of the way the High Priest who went into the "Holy of Holies" and sprinkled of the blood of the goat on which the lottery fell as "for the Lord" (Leviticus 16:8-9) and also as memorial of the second goat on which the lot fell as for the "Scapegoat".

The two goats together were collectively the shadow of the sacrifice of Jesus on the cross and bearing the sins of the sinner.

"And Aaron shall cast lots upon the two goats; one lot for the LORD, and the other lot for the scapegoat" (Leviticus 16:8 - KJV)

Darby's Translation of Leviticus 16:8 says: "And Aaron shall cast lots upon the two goats: one lot for Jehovah, and the other lot for Azazel".

The word "Azazel" is not clearly understood by anyone. The most accepted meaning is the same as "Scapegoat", which bore the confessed sins and went into the wilderness and died, never to return to the camp of Israel.

This "Scapegoat" is not Satan, which some believe it to be. The "Scapegoat" is the picture of Lord Jesus Christ, who bore our sins. This is highly misunderstood doctrine in Christian Theology.

Satan did not carry the sins of any one nor does anyone need to lay one's sin on Satan to take away into wilderness.

Some believe that it was Satan, who brought sin into the world and, therefore, Satan carries sin and dies in the wilderness, but this teaching is heresy. Jesus died for our sins and he bore our sins and died on the outskirts of city. Jesus is the salvation and his blood cleansed our sins.

"For he hath made him to be sin for us, who knew no sin; that we might be made the righteousness of God in him" 2 Corinthians 5:21.

The Old Testament sacrifices were not perfect in nature; yet it was not the mistake of Old Testament saints. It was ordained so by God.

It was not the mistake of God either to say that He gave imperfect first or perfect later; but it was the way to show that neither the blood of bulls nor of goats saved anybody, but only the blood of Jesus saved everyone who believed in Jesus as Savior. (Hebrews 10:4).

The atoning sacrifices in the Old Testament only

covered the sins, but the sins were not forgiven forever. They had to do it again the next year. That was a shadow of the things to come in future and the blood of Jesus Christ cleansed the sins of every one.

In the New Testament period we are privileged that we do not need to offer sacrifices. Christ died for our sake once and for all; and that was enough. Our part is to believe Jesus as our Savior and repent of our sins to him. Jesus is the mediator for us and He is our High priest.

"But Christ being come an high priest of good things to come, by a greater and more perfect tabernacle, not made with hands, that is to say, not of this building; Neither by the blood of goats and calves, but by his own blood he entered in once into the holy place, having obtained eternal redemption for us"(Hebrews 9:11-12)

"So Christ was once offered to bear the sins of many; and unto them that look for him shall he appear the second time without sin unto salvation". (Hebrews 9:28)

The blood of Jesus Christ cleansed the sins of the Old Testament Saints, and also the New Testament saints. Lord Jesus became the High Priest, after the order of Melchisedec, thus setting aside the imperfect sacrificial offerings of the Old Testament. Jesus was the Savior in the past, He is the Savior now, and He will be the Savior in future. Hebrews Chapters 9,10 and 11 detail the way Jesus became perfect sacrifice for all

HIS PRECIOUS BLOOD

But with the precious blood of Christ, as of a lamb without blemish and without spot: (1 Peter 1:19)

Jesus shed his blood on the cross for our sake that we may have everlasting life provided we believe in him. His blood shed was precious, without blemish and without any spot.

"But he was wounded for our transgressions; he was bruised for our iniquities: the chastisement of our peace was upon him; and with his stripes we are healed". (Isaiah 53:5)

The LORD spoke to Moses and to all the children of Israel that they shall not offer any living thing which was bruised, or crushed or broken, or cut or with any blemish. Any offering that had blemish was not acceptable to Him. (Exodus 12:5, Leviticus 22:17-33)

As was the blood of Jesus precious so was He Himself to the Father and to those who believe in him. Jesus was the living stone, who was rejected by men, but chosen of God.

Speaking at the Lord's Supper Jesus Christ says

about remembering his death. He then says to his disciples about eating his flesh and drinking his blood. The institution of the Lord's Supper is applicable to us also. Lord Jesus says that unless we eat the emblems that represent his flesh and drink from the cup that represents his blood we have no life. We were once far off but are brought near to his presence by the blood of Christ.

We are able to enter in his most holy place by the blood of Christ. He is the mediator of the new covenant and to the blood of sprinkling that speaks of better things than that of Abel.

The Father gave us peace through the death of our Lord Jesus Christ. Jesus was our shepherd and leads us every day. His death and blood that was shed enabled us to be shepherded by him who is our great shepherd. Jesus Christ's everlasting covenant was the cause for our reconciliation with the Father.

Our fellowship with one another is sustained when we walk in the light just as he was in the light. The blood of Jesus Christ cleanses us from all our sins. He washed us from our sins in his own blood. (Ref. John 6:53, Ephesians 2:13, Hebrews 10:19, Hebrews 12:24, Hebrews 13:20, 1 John 1:7, Revelation 1:5)

If you believe that Jesus Christ died for you, rose from the dead on the third day and later ascended into heaven your sins God will forgive your sins.

"Come now, and let us reason together, saith the LORD: though your sins be as scarlet, they shall be as white as snow; though they be red like crimson, they shall be as wool" (Isaiah 1:18)

"To whom coming, as unto a living stone, disallowed indeed of men, but chosen of God, and precious" (1 Peter 2:4 – (Cf. Ps 118:22; Isaiah 28:16; 53:5))

Psalmist prophesied about Jesus, that he was rejected but then he became the head stone of the corner (Ref. Psalms 118:22)

Peter wrote "Wherefore also it is contained in the scripture, Behold, I lay in Sion a chief corner stone, elect, precious: and he that believeth on him shall not be confounded". (1 Peter 2:6).

This was as prophesied in Isaiah 28:16 which reads as follows:

"Therefore thus saith the Lord GOD, Behold, I lay in Zion for a foundation a stone, a tried stone, a precious corner stone, a sure foundation: he that believeth shall not make haste"

Solomon's temple was the perfect Temple in Jerusalem and it is the true picture of the spiritual temple. The foundation of the Church was laid on

Jesus and he is the chief corner stone of the spiritual temple. For believers in Lord Jesus Christ he is precious but unto those who were disobedient and rejected him he became the corner stone on which the spiritual temple stands. On whomsoever this stone shall fall; it will grind him to powder and whosoever shall fall on this stone shall be broken. (Matthew 21:44)

Two references where Jesus was called the corner stone are: Matthew 21:42, and Acts 4:11-12. Jesus pointed to his own position questioning Jews if they have not read in prophesies that he was the stone which the builders rejected but became the corner stone.

Peter spoke of Lord Jesus Christ and said that the salvation is in Jesus alone and none else. Jesus, who was the stone which Jews rejected he became the corner stone to hold the spiritual temple in its position. (Acts 4:11-12)

"Unto you therefore which believe he is precious: but unto them which be disobedient, the stone which the builders disallowed, the same is made the head of the corner" (1 Peter 2:7)

For those who reject Lord Jesus Christ as savior he is a stone of stumbling, a rock of offence, and they will get hurt, but we are redeemed with precious blood of Lord Jesus Christ and not by corruptible things such as silver and gold and, therefore, we are as lively stones are built up spiritual house, an holy priesthood to offer spiritual sacrifices, acceptable to God by Jesus Christ.

"And a stone of stumbling, and a rock of offence, even to them which stumble at the word, being disobedient: whereunto also they were appointed". (1 Peter 2:8)

"Forasmuch as ye know that ye were not redeemed with corruptible things, as silver and gold, from your vain conversation received by tradition from your fathers" (1 Peter 1:18)

"Ye also, as lively stones, are built up a spiritual house, an holy priesthood, to offer up spiritual sacrifices, acceptable to God by Jesus Christ". (1 Peter 2:5)

Believing in Jesus will entail us not only to be partakers of his promises but also to be partakers of divine nature. The promises from God are exceedingly precious and they are infallible assurances to us. The promises that God made are in his power to grant to us, and he grants them to us as he pleases. (2 Peter 1:4)

CHPATER 7
SWORD OF THE SPIRIT

In spite of having all the pieces of protective armor we will be ineffective if we do not take refuge in the word of God, which is the two-edged sword. When Lord Jesus Christ was confronted with the devil He used the word of God as the weapon to defeat Satan. Jesus said "It is written" pointing to the Old Testament Scriptures to defeat Satan

When Jesus had fasted for forty days and fort nights he was hungry, and Satan taking undue advantage of His desire to have food, tempted Him saying "If thou be the Son of God, command that these stones be made bread"   But Jesus answered Satan   " It is written, Man shall not live by bread alone, but by every word that proceedeth out of the mouth of God"

Then, Satan takes Him into the Holy city and sets Him on a pinnacle of the temple and says to Him "If thou be the Son of God, cast thyself down: for it is written, He shall give his angels charge concerning thee: and in their hands they shall bear thee up, lest at any time thou dash thy foot against a stone" However, Jesus said unto him, It is written again, Thou shalt not tempt the Lord thy

God".

Again the devil takes Him to an exceeding high mountain, and shows Him the kingdoms of the world and says to Him "All these things will I give thee, if thou wilt fall down and worship me" However, Jesus said to the devil " Get thee hence, Satan: for it is written, Thou shalt worship the Lord thy God, and him only shalt thou serve"

Then devil left Him and the angels served Him.

If Jesus was to be tempted of Satan so much, and He quoted the Scripture to defeat him, how much more we should depend upon the Lord to be triumphant over Satan!   (Cf. Matthew 4:3-11, Psalm 91:11-12, Deuteronomy 8:3, Deuteronomy 6:16, Deuteronomy 6:13)

For the word of God is quick, and powerful, and sharper than any two-edged sword, piercing even to the dividing asunder of soul and spirit, and of the joints and marrow, and is a discerner of the thoughts and intents of the heart. (Hebrews 4:12)

THE DEVIL TEMPTS LORD JESUS

Matthew Chapter 3 ends with the details of Baptism of Jesus and with the Father testifying that the Son, Jesus, is His beloved Son, in whom He was much pleased.   It was the voice of the LORD Jehovah, the Almighty, who gave a testimony about the Son of God, who came into this world in the form of servant the likeness of a man.

What a great humility Lord Jesus Christ accepted that He relinquished the glory that He had with the Father to born in this world as man and in the womb of Mary, who was a virgin, and in whom the Father was much pleased. Mary was conceived of the Holy Ghost before she married Joseph. (Ref: Matthew 1:20, Matthew 3:17 and Philippians 2:7-11)

Matthew Chapter 4 starts with the details as to how Jesus was led into the wilderness to be tempted of the devil.   Jesus fasted for forty days and forty nights and He was hungry. Satan, the trickiest adversary of man, that old Dragon, who deceived Eve, tempts a man when he was weak and tired.

The tempter came to Jesus and said "If thou be the Son of God, command that these stones be made bread"

Bur Jesus quoted Scripture and said that man will not live by bread alone but by every word that goes out of the mouth of God. The scripture Jesus quoted was from Deuteronomy 8:3

"And he humbled thee, and suffered thee to hunger, and fed thee with manna, which thou

knewest not, neither did thy fathers know; that he might make thee know that man doth not live by bread only, but by every word that proceedeth out of the mouth of the LORD doth man live"

The devil, then, took Jesus up into the holy city, and placed Him on the highest spot of the temple and tempted Him saying if He was the Son of God He may cast down onto the ground because the Scripture says that the LORD will command the disciples to protect Him. The scripture the devil quoted was...

"For he shall give his angels charge over thee, to keep thee in all thy ways; They shall bear thee up in their hands, lest thou dash thy foot against a stone". (Psalms 91:11-12)

But Jesus said to the devil that *"it is written again, Thou shalt not tempt the Lord thy God" (Matthew 4:5-7)*

The Scripture Jesus quoted was from Deuteronomy 6:16 which reads...

"Ye shall not tempt the LORD your God, as ye tempted him in Massah"

The devil attempts third time and tempted Jesus to see if He would fall into his temptation. The devil took Him into an exceeding high mountain and showed Him all the kingdoms of the world and glory of them and said to Him that if He fell down and worshipped him, he would give all the world and that which is there in the world to the Lord.

Satan in his limited power is the king on this fleshly world filled with filth and sin. Lord Jesus was from above and He was pure, holy, and righteous without any blemish and without any sin in Him.

Surprisingly, Satan says the Holy Lord that he would give authority of this world to rule the world and sin. Lord Jesus Christ did not come into this world to be king of this world or to rule sin. He came into this world to save sinners and whoever accepts Him as savior will have everlasting life.

Then, Jesus said to the devil that it is written that the LORD alone is worthy of worship and He should only be worshipped.

The devil faced defeat and left Lord Jesus when He said to him "Get thee hence, Satan: for it is written, Thou shalt worship the Lord thy God, and him only shalt thou serve"   Satan left him and angels came and ministered to Him. (Ref: Matthew 4:11)

The scripture Lord Jesus quoted was from Deuteronomy 6:13 which reads...

"Thou shalt fear the LORD thy God, and serve him, and shalt swear by his name" (Deuteronomy 6:13)

There is one and only one God and the Bible points to Him as it is written in Deuteronomy 6:4 which reads..

"Hear, O Israel: The LORD our God is one LORD" (Deuteronomy 6:4)

If Satan could tempt the Son of God in human form in this world, then he could do much damage to our faith and tempt us, who are mere mortals, made of dust.

We need the strength of our Lord Jesus Christ and power of the Holy Spirit daily to overcome the temptations of Satan. Only by depending on Lord Jesus Christ we would be able to overcome satanic temptations.

The Bible says God does not tempt anybody but He provides a way for us to escape from the temptations; yet if he chooses to fall into devil's traps it is because we do not depend on Him, and do choose a sinful life.

There is penalty every sinner has to pay in this world before leaving this earth. Salvation is never lost, but sin leaves behind scars in man's life.

There hath no temptation taken you but such as is common to man: but God is faithful, who will not suffer you to be tempted above that ye are able; but will with the temptation also make a way to escape, that ye may be able to bear it. (1 Corinthians 10:13)

CHAPTER 8
PRAYER

Paul advises that In addition to fighting with the enemy with the sword, which is the word of God we need to pray constantly

"...Praying always with all prayer and supplication in the Spirit, and watching thereunto with all perseverance and supplication for all saints.

David's Psalm116 encourages believers to ponder life in retrospect and the deliverance the LORD wrought upon them from their distress, sin and iniquities.

Not once but several times in his life David was fleeing from his pursuers like Saul and then later in his life from his own son Absalom. In all the occasions when he was fleeing from his persecutors he depended on God for help and his prayers and supplications were answered.

Because David asked forgiveness from God He dealt with all his trials and tribulations compassionately and took care of them and forgave him.

The LORD called David, a man after His own heart. It is so precious to be called by God as a man after His own heart. David was not perfect in his life. His adultery with Bathsheba and killing of her husband Uriah had gone on record never to be erased.

He numbered his own army once pointing to the fact that his reliance on the LORD diminished. Yet, he was called a man of after God's own heart not because God approved his iniquities, sin and his pride but because David repented of his sin and sought mercy from the LORD.

David says he loved the LORD because He heard his voice and his supplications. The LORD inclined His ear to him and, therefore, he committed to call on the LORD as long as he lived.

He recollects that sorrows of death compassed him, and the pains of hell got hold of him. He called upon the name of the LORD to deliver his soul when he was in trouble and sorrow and the LORD delivered him because the LORD was gracious and merciful. David assures, thereafter, that the Lord preserves the humble.

The LORD was good to him when he confessed his sin to Him as we read in Psalm 51, It was when Nathan the prophet went to him and showed him how he has flawed in his walk with God. When the LORD gave him Kingship and the authority to rule over whole of Israel, he fell into his fleshly desire. David was highly remorseful of his sin and made available his psalm of confession to be sung by the chief musician aloud before the congregation.

David sought God's mercy and prayed to God to blot out his transgressions. He sought multitude of tender mercies and loving kindness from the LORD. David acknowledged his iniquity and prayed for his cleansing. He realized that by yielding to his fleshly desires he sinned against the LORD and done evil.

David also remembered the very condition of every man born on this earth. He says in sin did his mother conceive him and he was shaped in iniquity. This is the condition of every human being born on this earth. .

Behold, I was shapen in iniquity; and in sin did my mother conceive me. (Psalms 51:5)

Nevertheless, God looks at the heart of a man and searches his thoughts. Man is wicked in his very thoughts and unless he seeks the holy presence of the Lord in his heart he would slowly but surely slide into irretrievable situation of being in sin.

Apostle Paul writes that we all have sinned and fell short of the glory of God. The wages of sin is death but the gift of God is eternal life through

Jesus Christ our Lord. There is surely a way to be saved from sin and receive the gift of eternal life.

"That if thou shalt confess with thy mouth the Lord Jesus, and shalt believe in thine heart that God hath raised him from the dead, thou shalt be saved. For with the heart man believeth unto righteousness; and with the mouth confession is made unto salvation" Romans 10:29, 30

SACRIFICES

"For Christ is not entered into the holy places made with hands, which are the figures of the true; but into heaven itself, now to appear in the presence of God for us: Nor yet that he should offer himself often, as the high priest entereth into the holy place every year with blood of others" (Hebrews 9:24-25)

Usually man views his present status lightly unless he compares it with his previous status from where he was elevated.

He would give least importance to his present status if had forgotten the troubles and trials that he had undergone in rising up from his old status to the present status. He might think that he deserved all the blessings and they are all by his own virtue and his efforts.

Most of the Christians feel comfortable with the

freedom that they have in approaching the Father through Lord Jesus Christ without realizing that God was so unapproachable in the Old Testament period. The study of priests, high priest and the offerings and sacrifices that they had offer year after year will help Christians to appreciate the freedom they enjoy in Christ.

While the priests offered sacrifices several times a year on several occasions the high priest was authorized to enter the "Holy of Holies" only once a year to offer sin offering in a very meticulous method that God prescribed.

He risked his own life while making an entry into the Holy of Holies; first with incense, second with the blood of the Lord's goat. He then confessed the sins of the people by placing his hands on live goat If the high priest made any mistake in doing these ceremonies the result would be his instant death.

God gave specific instructions to Aaron, the high priest, through Moses, His servant and said violation of His instructions even to the minutest detail would invite Aaron's death. Every bit of instruction was to be followed meticulously without any negligence.

The LORD spoke to Moses, after the death of Nadab and Abihu, who were the sons of Aaron, the brother of Moses that Aaron should not enter not more than once a year into Holy of Holies where the mercy seat, which is upon the ark of the testament is located. If he committed any violation in this commandment, then he would die.

There was none to be present except the high priest within the whole tabernacle on the 'Day of Atonement' when the national repentance is made

"Ye also, as lively stones, are built up a spiritual house, an holy priesthood, to offer up spiritual sacrifices, acceptable to God by Jesus Christ". (1 Peter 2:5)

We have our way to the Father only through the sacrifice and our walk with God is by sanctification.

The sacrifices offered in the Old Testament period are the shadows of the perfect sacrifice seen in Lord Jesus Christ who died on our behalf bearing our sins upon Him in order that we may have salvation through Him. Jesus is the way, the truth and the life and no man can go the Father but by Him.

God met Moses first in the mountain and gave The Ten Commandments. Later, God told Moses about the construction of the Tabernacle and thereafter God met Moses in the "Holy of Holies" of the Tabernacle, which was also known as the 'Tent of Meeting'.

After God started meeting Moses in the Tabernacle the meeting on the mountain stopped completely. God was coming closer and closer to man and he presented Himself in the form of cloud over the mercy seat that was on the ark of the testament in the Holy of Holies in the Tabernacle.

God gave specific instructions to Moses about sacrifices, rituals, washings, convocations, liturgy, ceremonies and holy days, and warnings. The physical exercises depicted in the form of offering sacrifices and observances of rituals etc. teach us spiritual truths.

Whereas the children of Israel had Tabernacle where God met his servant Moses, we have the laws of God written through Lord Jesus Christ on our hearts. We are given the privilege to approach God at any time at any place. God did not establish any specific place for us to worship and we do not have rituals to observe.

The Lord said to the children of Israel through Moses that they should be holy as He was holy and he says the same to us also that we should be holy as he is holy.

"And ye shall be holy unto me: for I the LORD am

holy, and have severed you from other people, that ye should be mine". (Leviticus 20:26).

There was no way to approach God in the Old Testament period except through ;priests, who were mediators between God and men and through the sacrifices that they had to bring yearlong on various occasions.

The priests also had tough job to keep the fire under the altar burning always. Any error was not tolerated by God.

How privileged we are that all the believers are made priests through the sacrifice of Lord Jesus Christ and He became our high priest pleading on our behalf all the time.

Jesus said:

And if thine eye offend thee, pluck it out: it is better for thee to enter into the kingdom of God with one eye, than having two eyes to be cast into hell fire: (Mark 9:47)

Jesus is the Way, the truth, and the life. Holy Bible says God created man, in his own image and named him as Adam and God put him in a very comfortable place called 'the garden of Eden' and gave him a wife, whom Adam named as Eve.

God gave Adam and Eve all the freedom except

for eating the forbidden fruit, which Eve and Adam ate and brought sin into this world. In order to redeem mankind from their sin God sent his one and only son, Jesus Christ, who died for our sake, was buried, rose from the dead and ascended in to heaven. Salvation belongs to Lord Jesus Christ only.

GOD DELIVERS US FROM CURSE

"O LORD my God, in thee do I put my trust: save me from all them that persecute me, and deliver me" (Psalms 7:1)

According to the caption on Psalm 7 the psalm is written by David. In this Psalm is seen David's prayer to the LORD to save him from the curses that Cush the Benjamite hurled at him. Cush the Benjamite is identified as Shimei whose name is found in II Samuel 16:5-8

Shimei's curses hurled on David were of no small degree to be ignored of. They hit the core of the heart of the person at whom they are hurled. Hardly anybody except David would continue to hear them patiently and even allowing him to curse.

Shimei, the son of Gera, was from the family of Saul. Shimei cast stones at David and at all of his servants, all the people, and all the mighty men who were on his right hand and on his left. How daring he was that he threw stones at not only the King but also at so many others there. He could have been killed on the spot or arrested and punished later. His act seems to be one of the most foolish ones that any normal man could ever think of.

The words he uttered were so hurtful that not any man could forgive him or spare him. He said

"Come out, come out, thou bloody man, and thou man of Belial" Belial means worthless man. Shimei calls King David, a chosen one of the living God, as a worthless man. (Ref: 2 Samuel 16:7). In the New Testament Paul uses this word to point to Satan (2 Corinthians 6:15). Then he cursed saying

"The LORD hath returned upon thee all the blood of the house of Saul, in whose stead thou hast reigned; and the LORD hath delivered the kingdom into the hand of Absalom thy son: and, behold, thou [art taken] in thy mischief, because thou [art] a bloody man". 2 Samuel 16:8

King David relied on God on almost everything that he did in his life but on few occasions when he did not depend on God he failed miserably.

Here in this case David exhibits high degree of patience. He was the King over all Israel and was very powerful. He defeated many kings and was a man of wars and when Shimei cursed him he stood unmoved taking all the curses.

Abishai the son of Zeruiah heard the curses from Shimei and referring to him as 'dead dog' he sought permission from King David to go and take off his head but the King asked Abishai as to what he had to do with him. David went on saying that let Shimei curse him because he felt that the LORD allowed him to curse David.

David, who was a very powerful King over Israel, could have killed Shimei but he was gentle and handed him over to King Solomon to deal in his wisdom

Lord Jesus Christ was mocked at and was smitten for our salvation. He was blindfolded and was struck on his face and was insulted to prophesy. He suffered and bore our sin on Himself and whoever believes in Him and that God raised Him from the death will have everlasting life.

"And the men that held Jesus mocked him, and smote him. And when they had blindfolded him, they struck him on the face, and asked him, saying, Prophesy, who is it that smote thee? And many other things blasphemously spake they against him" (Luke 22:63-65)

VENGEANCE BELONGS TO GOD

"Give ear to my words, O LORD, consider my

meditation. Hearken unto the voice of my cry, my King, and my God: for unto thee will I pray" Psalm 5:1-2 In his Psalm 5, David seeks God's ears to hear his words and pleads that his petition may be heard.. Calling God as His king, David addresses his prayer to none but pointedly to Him alone, and pleads that his cry may be heard.

David was sure that Jehovah, who made him king over Israel, will hear his morning prayer because he directs it to none else but to Him alone. He looks up to the living God, who chose him as king over Israel. He directs his prayer to God of his fathers because He takes no pleasure in wickedness nor does He allow any evil to dwell near Him.

God detests every worker of iniquity, and therefore, He takes no pleasure in any of those evil workers and they will never be able to stand in His sight.

God abhors gossipers and destroys those who speak vanity. He abhors those who seek to shed blood of others and deceive men. But as for David, he promises God that He will come into the His house to worship Him looking towards His holy temple, in awe and fear, and enter into multitude of His mercies. His wish was that God may look at him.

God is faithful and just and His mercies will never

fail. He is slow to anger and longsuffering. However, as for the enemies of David, he says, there is no faithfulness in their mouths when they speak, and their hearts are highly wicked. Their throats, he says, are like open sepulcher, and they flatter with selfish motives to achieve their own selfish purposes.

David, as a king facing challenging situations, and with complex problems to rule the nation of Israel, prays to God to destroy the evil ones that they may fall by their own counsels.

Considering that his enemies rebelled against God, he seeks God to cast them out because of their huge number of transgressions. He commits evil doers and his enemies to God to take action. Vengeance belongs to God.

"To me belongeth vengeance and recompence; their foot shall slide in due time: for the day of their calamity is at hand, and the things that shall come upon them make haste. Deuteronomy 32:35

He prays for those who put their trust in the LORD that they may rejoice in Him and shout praises to him in joy because God defends them. His desire is that they may love the LORD and joyful in Him.

However, he is confident that the LORD God of Israel, Jehovah, will bless the righteous with favor and cover them with His shield.

If David depended on God for action against his enemies, then how much more we should depend on Him to help us out from troubles and problems!

"Dearly beloved, avenge not yourselves, but rather give place unto wrath: for it is written, Vengeance is mine; I will repay, saith the Lord" Romans 12:19.

CHAPTER 9
THE PRAYER OF JESUS

The prayer of Jesus, as we read in John Chapter 17, before he was betrayed for crucifixion has some significant truths. There are three divisions clearly seen in the prayer of Jesus. Firstly, he prayed for himself, secondly he prayed for his disciples, thirdly he prayed not for the world but for those who believe on him through the message of his disciples.

John Chapter 17:1-5 contain Jesus' prayer for himself, John 17:6-10 contain Jesus' prayer for his disciples and John 17:11-26 contain Jesus' prayer for those who believe on Jesus through the message of his disciples.

In the prayer for himself he glorified the Father and said that he has glorified the Father and that he may be glorified likewise. Jesus lifted up his eyes to heaven and said to the Father that hour is come and prayed that the Son may glorify the Father. Jesus says that the Father gave power to the Son over all flesh that the Son may give eternal life to as many as the Father gave to the Son. Jesus prays that those who believe in him may have the life eternal that they might know the Father, who is the only true God, and Jesus

Christ whom the Father sent. Jesus had earlier said the Father and the Son are one. "I and my Father are one" (John 10:30) and John 14:6 reads "Jesus saith unto him, I am the way, the truth, and the life: no man cometh unto the Father, but by me". (John 14:6)

Jesus prayed to the Father that he may be glorified in the Father with the glory that the Son had with the Father before the world was. (Cf. John 17:1-5) He continued his prayer and says that he glorified the Father and finished the work that the Father assigned to him.

Later, his disciple Peter explained about the glory that the Son of God, Lord Jesus Christ relinquished and came down to this earth in the form of servant and made in the likeness of men. Lord Jesus Christ was in the form of God, and yet he did not think it robbery to be equal to be with God and made himself of no reputation. "He humbled himself and became obedient unto death, even the death of the cross".

Jesus came down to this earth to save sinners. The Father exalted him and gave him the name above every name "that at the name of Jesus every knee should bow, of the things in heaven, and things in earth, and things under the earth". Every tongue will confess him that Jesus Christ is the Lord to the glory of the Father. (Cf. Philippians 2:6-11)

At the trial before Pilate Jesus was asked questions. Pilate asked him if Jesus was the King of the Jews. In answer Jesus asked Pilate if he was asking this question on his own or did somebody asked him to inquire about Jesus. Pilate vehemently asserted that he was not Jew and that the nation of Jesus and the chief priests delivered him to Pilate.

Jesus said that his kingdom is not of this world, but his kingdom is yet to come. Pilate continues his questions and asked Jesus if Jesus was the king of the Jews. Jesus said that Pilate had said so and for this reason he was born and for this reason he came into the world that he should bear witness unto the truth.

Jesus said that everyone who is of the truth will hear his voice. When people desired that Barabbas be released in preference to Jesus Pilate released Barabbas and scourged Jesus (Cf. John 18:33-40)

"Then Pilate therefore took Jesus, and scourged him". (John 19:1)

Pilate questioned Jesus as to where Jesus was from and Jesus did not give him any answer. Pilate then boasted saying the he had the power to crucify Jesus or to realize him. But then, Jesus said to Pilate that he had no power over Jesus except it was given to him from above. (John

19:9-11) The people cried there that Jesus be crucified

"Then answered all the people, and said, His blood be on us, and on our children". (Matthew 27:25)

Pilate then, delivered Jesus to be crucified.

"Then delivered he him therefore unto them to be crucified. And they took Jesus, and led him away". (John 19:16)

JESUS DIED IN OUR STEAD

"For when we were yet without strength, in due time Christ died for the ungodly" (Romans 5:6)

Jesus had embarrassing situations earlier when Jews tried to harm Him, but no one could do any harm to him, because the due time for Him to die on behalf of us had not yet come (Ref. John 7:30).

Until the determined hour was come no one could do any harm to Jesus, and when the appointed hour was come, He was taken into custody by the chief priests and elders who took counsel against Him to put Him to death.

"And Jesus answered them, saying, The hour is come, that the Son of man should be glorified" (John 12:23)

The events on the day of trial, as before the trial, and after the trial of Jesus, and the plan of man's redemption were determined by the eternal counsel of the Almighty God.

"And all that dwell upon the earth shall worship him, whose names are not written in the book of life of the Lamb slain from the foundation of the world" (Revelation 13:8)

All the disciples of Jesus scattered away, from the scene when Jesus was arrested, and left Him all alone in fulfillment of the prophecy by the prophet Zechariah. (Ref. Zechariah 13:7). Peter denied Jesus three times in fulfillment of the prophecy from Jesus. Judas Iscariot betrayed Jesus in fulfillment of the prophecy by the prophet Zechariah (Ref. Zechariah 11:12-13)

"Awake, O sword, against my shepherd, and against the man that is my fellow, saith the LORD of hosts: smite the shepherd, and the sheep shall be scattered: and I will turn mine hand upon the little ones" (Zechariah 13:7)

While Peter repented and chose to serve the Lord, Judas Iscariot betrayed Jesus and committed suicide.

The chief priests and the elders of the people delivered Jesus in the morning to the governor, Pontius Pilate, for executing Jesus to death. If only they said Jesus violated their religious laws, Pilate would have let Jesus go even before the trial began, because Roman Government had no authority to deal with cases related to religious laws. Knowing this well, the Jews leveled false charges against Jesus; and the charges were related to treason, insurrection against Government.

It was only few years ago before the crucifixion of Jesus that Roman Government stripped Jews from their power to inflict Capital punishment on those who broke their religious laws.

It was because they did not have any powers over Him, neither did Roman Government, unless they were given from heaven above, no one by his power could execute Jesus. Ultimately, after the trial of Jesus was over, He was found innocent.

There was nothing, He did in His lifetime, which made Him worthy of death penalty. Even secular law provides chance for the accused to be acquitted of unproved charges, but in the case of Jesus, Pontius Pilate, who boasted that he had the power to execute or release Jesus, delivered innocent Jesus to be crucified.

Because it was the purpose of Jesus to die for men in their stead, He did not plead for his innocence or acquittal.

All that Jesus did was good for mankind; such as healing the sick, casting away the devils from those who were afflicted by them. He taught repentance and the way to receive everlasting life. The chief priests, the Jews and the elders of people feared that Jesus would become prominent among them, and would replace them in power.

Therefore, they leveled false charges against Him and were determined to see that He was put to death. They even cried that the blood of Jesus to be upon them and their children. Pilate found no fault in Jesus. Pilate's wife was troubled in a dream about the illegal trial of Jesus and cautioned him; yet he delivered Jesus into their hands to do what they desired to do.

The last attempt Pilate made was to release either a criminal, named Barabbas or Jesus according to their choice, and they preferred Barabbas to be released instead of Jesus. What a choice they made! T

hey preferred to kill Jesus, who was good to them all His life, and to be robbed by Barabbas, the criminal. They made a choice that the blood of Jesus to be on them, and their children, at the cost of some secular benefits. They preferred lies instead of truth saying Jesus resorted to insurrection.

"The Son of man" would have gone as it was written about Him.   The tragedy was that they invited troubles for them, and preferred to receive punishment from God.

It is not that we loved God first but He loved us first, and that is the reason why He sent His one and only begotten Son into this world to die in our stead. He died for our sake and was buried. His body did not see corruption and He rose on the third day and after forty days He ascended into heaven.

"And being found in fashion as a man, he humbled himself, and became obedient unto death, even the death of the cross". (Philippians 2:8)

CHAPTER 10
WE PREACH CHRIST CRUCIFIED

Our God always resisted and hated anyone who worshipped idols, and other gods. He will not share or give away His glory to anyone. He has shown his mighty power before Egyptians and their king Pharaoh, who took delight in worshipping various gods, such as 'frog gods', 'lice' gods etc.

God showed that he is mightier than any other gods by giving Egyptians plenty of frogs, plenty of lice that they hated them. These gods who are man-made idols and whom God wanted us to hate had become gods of Aaron and the children of Israel several times while they were on their way to the Promised Land.

God delivered them from Egyptians and led them through the wilderness providing them food, light, shelter. He made them to cross the Red Sea on foot on the dry land when waters separated and stood like walls on either side of their path.

In spite of these miracles God had done in their

lives, they children of Israel faltered several times. Whenever they faltered God gave them over to their desires and allowed them to suffer until they repented and returned to God for help.

God never wanted them to be cast away totally, but subjected them to chastisement time and again in order that they may learn to be faithful to him.

Stephen speaks of ingratitude that the children of Israel had shown towards Jehovah, who delivered them from the bondage of slavery under Pharaoh. The children of Israel made for themselves a calf in those days and not only offered sacrifices to it but rejoiced in the god that they have made by their own hands (Acts 7:41)

They have shown ingratitude towards to the living God, who spoke to Moses on the Mount Sinai and gave them the Ten Commandments to obey. When there was delay in Moses coming down from the Mount Sinai, Aaron, elder brother of Moses, made a molten calf for them to worship.

Aaron was chosen by God to be mouth piece of Moses to speak to the children of Israel, but he showed allegiance to the god made by their own hands. The god that does not speak a word to them, the god that does not help them in any way has become their rock of refuge, who they thought would lead them in the wilderness.

The children of Israel have shown this ingratitude not once but several times. Then God turned them over to their own desires to worship the host of heaven. (Amos 5:25-27, Acts 7:42).

God showed compassion on them when they repented of their failure and sin, but then continued to fall again and again. God chastised them time and again whenever they disobeyed him and forgave them whenever they repented of their failures and sin.

Stephen calls the descendants of the patriarchs as "Ye stiff-necked and uncircumcised in heart and ears, ye do always resist the Holy Ghost: as your fathers did, so do ye" (Acts 7:51)

It is time we introspect ourselves and return to God.

CAN WE CONFINE GOD TO A PLACE?

Recounting the worship of idols, and sacrifices of beasts and human bodies to them by the descendants of Patriarchs, whom Stephen refers as 'your fathers', he says that they carried the Tabernacle on their way to the Promised Land, but had developed an idea of confining God to a place and temple.

When Solomon built the temple and some of the elements of the Tabernacle were placed in it, the children of Israel thought that God can be confined to a place.

Stephen was exposing their utter misunderstanding of God when they blamed him that he was speaking against their holy place and the commandments of Moses that allegedly he was trying to break and teaching people to break.

Stephen exposes their folly that they gave their devotion to the host of heaven, and offered sacrifices with delight to the idols.

He says that they took up tabernacle of Moloch, a sun-god, and Remphan, a moon or star-god, and worshipped them. He says, that after worshipping such idols they thought the living God can also be confined to a place or to a temple. That was their understanding after Solomon built the temple.

The offering of the worship in the Tabernacle and building of Solomon's temple was in the plan of God, and He wanted the children of Israel to obey and keep his commandments. Yet, the understanding about confining God a place or temple was in error.

Stephen, therefore, questions them if it was possible to confine God to a temple built with hands! The LORD said that Heaven was his throne and earth was his footstool and who could make him dwell in a place like Temple.

Thus saith the LORD, The heaven is my throne, and the earth is my footstool: where is the house that ye build unto me? and where is the place of my rest? (Isaiah 66:1)

Heaven is my throne, and earth is my footstool: what house will ye build me? saith the Lord: or what is the place of my rest? (Acts 7:49)

Stephen's point in defense against their false allegations was that they did not have perfect understanding about the temple, and he never said that he would destroy the temple nor did he speak blasphemous words against the holy place or the Law of Moses. Peradventure even if he spoke such words as they alleged him of, he was not in error.

The elders and scribes lodged false allegations against Stephen that he said Jesus of Nazareth would destroy their holy place and change their customs that they derived from Moses. Stephen was innocent, yet he spoke boldly and charged them they were stiff-necked and persecuted their fathers.

HUMILITY

Lord Jesus was in the form of God and did not think it robbery to be to equal with God, but made himself of no repute, took the form of servant, and became like a man and dwelt among us. He was born of the Virgin Mary, by the works of Holy Spirit, and was laid in a manger.

He was raised in a poor family. His earthly parents offered turtle doves as offerings (Luke 2:24), which was a provision made for poor and those, who could not offer bull or goat as sacrifice as per Old Testament Law.

In Colossians 1st Chapter verses 15 to 17, there is a clear description that Jesus the creator. He is the image of the invisible God, the first born of every creature, and by him were all things created; yet we see that he took the form of man for our sake. He testified, in Luke 9:58 how poor he was on this earth.

In the book of Hosea the pathetic condition of Israel is seen. Israel, who had been blessed and to whom were the blessings and covenants given, continually fell from the presence of the Lord.

In the sight of the Lord, who asked Hosea to marry a prostitute, Israel was similar to Prostitute, dishonest with her infidelity. God, who was like husband to them had to see her deviation from the honesty and loyalty, had to chastise them time and again. The Lord goes on to say that they are not his people, and he is not their God. He was like a frustrated husband trying to bring them to the path of salvation, yet they erred time and again. This was the reason, why God had to extend salvation to the Gentiles, thus making Jews and Gentiles one in Christ.

It was not a mystery that the Gentiles should be saved but one mystery was certainly there that God would form Church consisting of Jews and Gentiles, and that Church is above Jews and Gentiles. This purpose was hidden in God until it was revealed to us in Ephesians 2nd Chapter. The Church is the body of Christ. In this Church are no differences as to who is Jew and who is Gentile, but everyone has similar status.

In this Church is seen no more distinction of earthly differences of race, ethnicity, clan, color, and nationality. It is the blood of Jesus that saves a man from being condemned to death and eternal destruction. It is the water that Jesus gives that becomes living water for the sinner. It is the life that Jesus gives to sinner that becomes eternal life.

God in his mercy and love for us quickened us in spirit together with Christ and by grace we are saved. He has given us the privilege to be seated together in heavenly places in Christ Jesus. Faith in him alone saved us and not of any good works in us or by us. If the salvation is by works, then anybody could boast of himself/herself by doing good works that he is worthy to receive salvation by himself, and of his good works. This renders the sacrifice of Jesus of null effect.

The very purpose of Jesus coming into this world was to bear on himself, the sins of the world so that whoever believes in him could be saved.

If good works of any man could save him, then Christ need not have come to this world. There is a fundamental error in believing that good works of any man would save him from his sins.

We are his workmanship, created in Christ Jesus unto good works. This was in the plan of God even before the foundation of the world. The good works of a man will not save him but in Christ Jesus we will do good works as a result of having the fruit of the Holy Spirit.

We were without Christ, and aliens from the commonwealth of Israel. We had no hope of having salvation but in the blood of Jesus Christ we are made one.

All this was took place because Jesus became a sacrifice on our behalf, when he took upon himself, our curse, our sin and shed his precious blood upon the cross of Calvary. The salvation is received by his 'grace' through faith in him that he died and rose for our sake, and by accepting his as 'Lord '. He offered himself on the cross so that we may have riches in him.

The earthly riches are not true riches. What if a man earns whole earth his soul? We are saved by his precious blood and not of any of our works. We are not purchased by gold and/or silver, but by the blood of Jesus, who paid it as price for our salvation.

PROPITIATION

The Word, "Propitiation" occurs in New Testament, which means, at this context, in Scriptures, the sacrifice rendered in order to cover the sins. Jesus became propitiation for us to make reconciliation, so that we, who were fallen, once are made righteous.

He became propitiation for our sins; and not only ours but for the sins of the whole world. In that the love of God is seen; he loved us first and he sent his One and Only begotten Son, for our sake. In Old Testament the blood of the bullock was taken and sprinkled.

The priest sprinkled it with his finger upon the mercy seat eastward; and seven times before the mercy seat. But, when Christ became propitiation for us, he became an high priest of good things to come, by a perfect tabernacle, which is not made of hands, and not of the blood of the bullocks of goats and calves but by his own blood.

Christ entered in once into the holy place, having obtained eternal redemption for us. Jesus Christ has thus become the mediator on behalf of us, inasmuch as his blood was without any blemish.

We have Jesus Christ as our high Priest, who was in all points tempted like any one of us (Hebrews4:14-16). We have, therefore, every right to come to the throne of grace, so that we may obtain mercy, find grace to help in time of need.

Romans 5:13 For until the law sin was in the world: but sin is not imputed when there is no law.

REDEMPTION

Redemption, in the context of New Testament doctrine, is getting something back for the price paid; in other words, setting forth a sinner free from the bondage of sin with the price paid by Jesus Christ on the cross.

It is to deliver by paying price. There are three things that take place in the process of redemption. It is buying something that was under bondage.

It was setting free from the bondage and it is freeing from that bondage. This is what exactly what Christ did on the cross on behalf of sinner. Every man is under the bondage of sin from the time he is born in the womb of his mother. Scripture says, there is no one righteous, and anyone who does not accept this fact is making the writer of the Scripture a liar -- '1 John 1:10 If we say that we have not sinned, we make him a liar, and his word is not in us. '

The man under the bondage of sin needs deliverance. This is what Christ did on the cross by dying in the stead of sinner taking upon himself the sins of the sinner fulfilling the law.

Every man, who is freed from the bondage, needs to be delivered just as a product or animal is taken out of the market place and freed.

This is what Jesus did by freeing from the bondage of sin, and delivering us from the penalty of sin, which is death. Our bodies perish and we rise in glory with glorified bodies.

While the bodies still lie in the grave and perish, the soul of a believer is eternally present with the Lord Jesus Christ right from the movement is gives up his earthly life.

Romans 7:13 *"Was then that which is good made death unto me? God forbid. But sin, that it might appear sin, working death in me by that which is good; that sin by the commandment might become exceeding sinful"*

The law pointed out sin, but the grace delivered us from the bondage of sin. Accepting Jesus as the Lord and Savior will set a sinner free from the bondage of sin, and entitles him to have eternal life.

THE LOVE OF GOD

"Who shall lay anything to the charge of God's elect? It is God that justifieth. Who is he that condemneth? It is Christ that died, yea rather, that is risen again, who is even at the right hand of God, who also maketh intercession for us. Who shall separate us from the love of Christ? shall tribulation, or distress, or persecution, or famine, or nakedness, or peril, or sword? As it is written, For thy sake we are killed all the day long; we are accounted as sheep for the slaughter. Nay, in all these things we are more than conquerors through him that loved us. For I am persuaded, that neither death, nor life, nor angels, nor principalities, nor powers, nor things present, nor things to come, Nor height, nor depth, nor any other creature, shall be able to separate us from the love of God, which is in Christ Jesus our Lord ".

Adam transgressed God's commandment when he ate of the fruit of the knowledge of good and evil brought to him by the woman after she was deceived by the serpent. The serpent was 'more subtil than any beast of the field which the LORD God had made '.

Adam brought upon himself and his posterity the condemnation of death. It was the consequence of imputation of guilt to him because he transgressed the commandment of God. Man needed reconciliation and forgiveness.

Jesus, the Son of God came into this world, took upon himself man's sin, died on the cross. Jesus, whom God hath raised up, having loosed the pains of death because it was not possible that he should be holden of it. (Acts 2 :24). Jesus ascended into heaven and is now seated on the right of the Majesty.

Whosoever believes this fact will have eternal life. For if by one man's offence death reigned by one; much more they which receive abundance of grace and of the gift of righteousness shall reign in life by one, Jesus Christ. Romans 5 :17

Apostle Paul writes in Galatians 3:24 "Wherefore the law was our schoolmaster to bring us unto Christ, that we might be justified by faith". The Law was given to Moses and for those under Old Testament Covenant. The believer in Christ is not asked here to disregard the Law, but is asked not to be under its bondage, because law cannot save any person. The law brings a sinner in to condemnation.

A New Testament believer is not under the bondage of law. The Scriptures say that if anyone is bent upon keeping the law he needs to keep all the commandments, which is virtually impossible.

The message is clearly not to be disobedient to law or disregard the law. The message is clearly that of emphasizing the fact that it is impossible for any human to keep the law that was given by God, and be justified; the justification was possible only through the blood that was shed on the cross, of Jesus.

Quoting Scriptures just as the tempter did the Scriptures when he tested Jesus (Matt 4th Ch.), Pharisees and Sadducees, highly educated elite and religious leaders of Jesus's time attempted to trap Jesus several times by the words.

One such attempt was by quoting from Deuteronomy 25:5-10 about the law of Moses, and said to Jesus, that according to law, 'if a man die having no children his brother shall marry his wife and raise up seed unto his brother'.

Their attempt was to take advantage of this scripture and posed a question to him that if seven brothers attempt in vain to raise an offspring from a single woman, whose wife would she be in resurrection. (Matt. 22:24-30)

Jesus understood their motif and replied to them that they do err in being unaware of scriptures and the power of God. He said, 'But as touching the resurrection of the dead, have ye not read that which was spoken unto you by God, saying, I am the God of Abraham, and the God of Isaac, and the God of Jacob?

God is not the God of the dead, but of the living' Matthew 22:31-32. Further, He said that in resurrection no one will marry nor anyone is given in marriage, but they all will be like angels in heaven.

Sadducees then tried to trap Jesus in another question. One of them was a lawyer, who asked him as to which commandment in the law was great. Jesus answered and said to them, 'Thou shalt love the Lord thy God with all thy heart, and with all thy soul, and with all thy mind. This is the first and great commandment. And the second is like unto it, Thou shalt love thy neighbour as thyself. On these two commandments hang all the law and the prophets'.

Jesus, knowing their thoughts and intentions said to them that he has not come to destroy law or the prophets but to fulfill. He also said that the law and the prophets were until John and then onward 'the kingdom of God is preached'.

Warning them, Jesus said that the deeds and works, which they consider as righteousness in their own eyes according to their own understanding does not save them. They, who try to justify themselves before men, but God knows their hearts and judges them.

They consider themselves as highly esteemed but they are abomination in the sight of God. (Luke 16:15-17). Jesus affirmed that heaven and hearth will pass but one title of the law will not fail.

Jesus asked them why were they angry at him when he healed a man on Sabbath, while they who profess Sabbath should be a day of rest fail to observe that day and circumcise on that day. Is it not worth considering the fact that 'In the end of the Sabbath, as it began to dawn toward the first day of the week, came Mary Magdalene and the other Mary to see the sepulcher'. Matthew 28:1

The Sabbath was over, and on the first day of the week, Jesus rose from the dead. Jesus also said 'For the Son of man is Lord even of the sabbath day' Matthew 12:8

The Old Testament Law was abolished when Jesus was crucified on the cross. The Old Testament Law

was nailed to the cross as we read in Colossians 2 :14 "Blotting out the handwriting of ordinances that was against us, which was contrary to us, and took it out of the way, nailing it to his cross "
Romans 10 :4

"For Christ is the end of the law for righteousness to every one that believeth ".

If anyone still believes in the Old Testament Laws, then Christ is no effect to him inasmuch as the Scripture says, 'whosoever of you are justified by the law; ye are fallen from grace '.

All those, who were in Old Testament period, have seen that no one could keep the law perfectly.

The law always pointed to the sin, and showed the guilt of a person. It always demanded works, and condemned. Even before the foundation of the world God knew that man cannot keep the law, and needs a savior.

The law was given to him to show in the future days to come that after the law was given and after it is seen that men have failed to keep the law, man should be made to understand that he needs grace and nothing but grace.

No amount of good works could save a person; but the salvation is received by sinner only by laying faith in Jesus and faith alone in him saves a person.

More references : Jeremiah 31 :31-34, 1 Corinthians 10 :1-4, Romans 15 :4, Galatians 5 :4, Romans 7 :4-6, Ephesians 2 :15

Romans 3:25 Whom God hath set forth to be a propitiation through faith in his blood, to declare his righteousness for the remission of sins that are past, through the forbearance of God

JUSTIFICATION

1 Corinthians 1:30 But of him are ye in Christ Jesus, who of God is made unto us wisdom, and righteousness, and sanctification, and redemption

Justification is the declaration that our Lord and Savior Jesus Christ makes before the Father about a sinner, who believes in Jesus Christ and accepts him as his personal Savior.

The sinner, who confesses him as the 'Lord' is justified by him as righteous because Christ has borne the sins of sinner on the cross of Calvary and made him righteous.

The justification originates in and through the grace. It is by grace through faith in him that a sinner is saved. No amount of good works can save a person, nor can justify him as righteous before God.

Romans 3:24 "Being justified freely by his grace through the redemption that is in Christ Jesus".

It is judicial act that Jesus has performed on the cross. He paid the price for the redemption of sinner. He died in the stead of a sinner. That is how he justifies the sinner as righteous before the Father.

All that a sinner needs to do is to accept the fact that Jesus Christ has died on the cross in his stead and rose from the dead on the third day.

It is by faith in Jesus as the redeemer that a sinner is saved and no charge is laid against him, irrespective of what gross sin he/she has committed. Every sin, except blasphemy of Holy Spirit, is pardonable by God. Christ has established the law by taking upon himself the penalty of sin, which is death.

As believers in Christ we have blessed hope that after death we will have glorified bodies that are not made of hands but that which will be with the Lord eternally in the heavens.

The body that we have now is made of dust and we groan in this body to be clothed to hide nakedness, in contrast to the glorified bodies that we will have in heaven. Our bodies are made with the dust from this earth and, therefore, suffer sickness and decay in contrast to the glorified bodies that do not suffer any sickness or decay in eternity.

This is the reason why we believers are happy to be absent in this body so that we can be present eternally with the Lord, and, therefore, we do not fear death. In this body we labor to earn for our life on this earth, but in eternity we are blessed with the rewards that our Lord gives us for the works that we have done for him on this earth.

Jesus died for our sake, and rose again from the dead giving us the blessed hope that even though we die we will rise once in glorified bodies.

"So also is the resurrection of the dead. It is sown in corruption; it is raised in incorruption : (1 Corinthians 15 :42)

"Therefore if any man be in Christ, he is a new creature: old things are passed away ; behold, all things are become new ". (2 Corinthians 5 :17)

"The Price is already paid for"

John 19:30 When Jesus therefore had received the vinegar, he said, It is finished: and he bowed his head, and gave up the ghost.

This is one of the seven sayings of Jesus when he was on the cross of Calvary. He was despised and rejected by man

This is the fulfillment of prophesy that is written in Isaiah 53:4-7 "Surely he hath borne our griefs, and carried our sorrows: yet we did esteem him stricken, smitten of God, and afflicted. But he was wounded for our transgressions, he was bruised for our iniquities: the chastisement of our peace was upon him; and with his stripes we are healed.

All we like sheep have gone astray; we have turned every one to his own way; and the LORD hath laid on him the iniquity of us all. He was oppressed, and he was afflicted, yet he opened not his mouth: he is brought as a lamb to the slaughter, and as a sheep before her shearers is dumb, so he openeth not his mouth".

He was led like a lamb to be slaughtered. His hands and feet were nailed. He was numbered with the transgressors his death.

Isaiah 53:10 "Yet it pleased the LORD to bruise him; he hath put him to grief: when thou shalt make his soul an offering for sin, he shall see his seed, he shall prolong his days, and the pleasure of the LORD shall prosper in his hand." His blood was paid as price for our redemption.

There was nothing more, nor is anything more to be done by any person for receiving salvation. It is just the faith in him as Lord and Savior that is required of a person to have everlasting life. Jesus took upon himself our infirmities and sin so that we may have everlasting life. It pleased the Father to bruise him so that we may receive salvation. There is no price attached to that invaluable gift that is given to us. The price is already paid for.

Getting entangled with law and with the thought that they need to do something to be saved, is tantamount to be under the yoke of bondage, he says. About, circumcision, he condemns it and says that if anyone is of the belief that circumcision is necessary for salvation or for justification, the obsession of such thought will not profit them and Christ and his blood is of nothing to them.

Everyone, who is circumcised, becomes debtor to the whole law and Christ and his sacrifice has nothing for him. We are reckoned as righteous only by faith in Jesus and by his grace. Neither circumcision nor un-circumcision avails anything to a believer in Christ.

Walking in the Spirit and hatred of lust of the flesh are necessary on the part of a believer to lead a holy life. One great truth a believer has to understand is that flesh lusts against the Spirit and the Spirit against the flesh and these are contrary to each other. If we are of the Spirit and are led by the Spirit we are not under the law and would not yield to the desires of the flesh.

After having known of the love of God through

His one only begotten son, Jesus, why would we turn yet unto beggarly elements like observing the days, months, times and years, and be subject again to be under the bondage of the law? When the price for our sin and redemption is already paid for, why would we turn again to work for our salvation by ourselves?

Salvation is available free of cost; the price is already paid for. All that is needed on the part of sinner is to believe that Jesus paid the price of his sin on the cross, and that he needs to believe in his/her heart this fact and accept him as his/her personal Savior.

RECONCILIATION

The contemptuous wall of separation that divided Gentiles from Jews on the reason that Jews kept the law and Gentiles, who did not keep the law, was once for all removed when Jesus died for us on the cross.

The separation between Jews and Gentiles was abolished with the crucifixion of Jesus Christ. Jesus having kept the law has abolished in 'flesh the enmity, even the law of commandments contained in ordinances'.

By his own blood Jesus reconciled man with God, and Jews with Gentiles making man a new. Jesus reconciled man unto God in one body by the cross. He made Jews and Gentiles as one body by shedding his blood on the cross. The barrier that separated Gentiles from Jews that the former did not keep the law, and had Jews in derision for keeping the ordinances of the law, was once for all removed.

Through Jesus, who is the way, the truth and the life, we have access by Spirit unto the Father. Therefore, we are no longer 'strangers and foreigners but fellow citizens with the saints and of the household of God'.

Jesus says 'Come unto me, all ye that labour and are heavy laden, and I will give you rest'.

He said that children should not be forbidden to come unto him. By making Jews and Gentiles as one body and by breaking the 'middle wall of partition' he made peace between God and man, Jews and Gentiles. That is the reconciliation.

Jesus made peace through his blood that was shed on the cross so as to reconcile all things unto himself, irrespective of their belonging to earth or to heaven.

Therefore, everything belongs to God, who has reconciled us to himself by Jesus Christ and he has given us the ministry of reconciliation. In order that our trespasses may not be imputed to us, he has committed unto us the word of reconciliation.

God was in Christ when He was reconciling us unto Himself.

[References: Matthew 11:28, Matthew 19:14, 2 Corinthians 5:18 and 19, Colossians 1:20, Ephesians 2:14-19]

EYE OF A NEEDLE

James comes down very harshly on rich men asking them to weep and howl as they depend too much on their worldly wealth rather than the wealth in heaven. He calls the riches on this earth are 'cankered' and says that their stored wealth, gold and silver, would rust.   They think that these metals would help them in every situation.

In the first place, they are accountable as to the ways they have adopted to gather their wealth. Was it not by denying the laborers their due share of wages, and/or was it not by saving by fraud? They condemned and killed the just? They have lived a life of pleasure on this earth and failed to accumulate wealth in heaven.   The result would be that they end up as paupers in heaven.. (James 5)

Apostle Paul writes to Timothy that we brought nothing into this world, and it is sure that we will not carry anything out from this world when we leave this earth. He says, it is enough if we have food and raiment. Those, who are excessively rich fall into temptations and snare themselves unto damnation. He shows us a great reality that the root cause for all evil is money and desiring to become rich.

There was a rich man, who went to Jesus and kneeling before him asked him, what he should do inherit eternal life. The rich man called Jesus 'Good master'.

He thought that Jesus was just a human teacher. Jesus knew his hypocritical thoughts and knew that he would not give away his wealth to anybody. When Jesus asked the rich man to keep the commandments he said that he was keeping the commandments from his childhood.

Jesus said to him to sell all that he had, distribute it to the poor, take up the cross, and follow him in order to have riches in heaven.

The rich man was disappointed because he had great possessions. Jesus, then said, 'It is easier for a camel to go through the eye of a needle, than for a rich man to enter into the kingdom of God'. (Mark 10:17-25)

What then is it is sin to have possessions and riches on this earth? No, Abraham was rich, David was rich, Solomon was rich, Job was rich and many others, yet they all gave glory to the living God, and blessed them with true riches.

Paul gives a very touching advise that man of God should flee from these worldly things and seek righteousness, goodness, faith, love, patience, and meekness. We should fight a good fight of faith in pursuit of eternal life and rewards in heaven. (Cf. 1 Timothy 6th Chapter)

We have God who is eternal and living One, the One who offered His own son, Jesus Christ, for the remission of our sins; and in his blood are our sins cleansed. He is the one asking us to invest in his eternal kingdom and wants you and me to test him to see if our barns do not overflow with riches!

Depending upon God and remembering him, who gives us power and wealth and establishes his covenant that he swore to our fathers, will be the wisest thing we can think of doing rather than risking our money in winning games by chance.

Did we ever consider the biggest lottery we can play is to depend upon our God? Deuteronomy 8:18 says,

"But thou shalt remember the LORD thy God: for it is he that giveth thee power to get wealth, that he may establish his covenant which he sware unto thy fathers, as it is this day."

Our Lord is the provider and he provides money for you and me for all our genuine needs. Psalmist acknowledges that he has not seen the child of God begging for bread.

What is wealth? Do we take literal meaning of the word, "Wealth". Does wealth mean to us possessing immovable property, beautiful cars, and a big bank balance? What if God takes away health, and gives us big bank balance! Does it mean we are rich? Let us take the word of Jesus Christ to heart, that it is easier for a camel to get through the eye of a needle than for a rich man to enter the Kingdom of God.

There is nothing wrong to be rich and acquire riches in righteous way, but it is certainly wrong to misuse our resources to acquire wealth by fraudulent methods. The property inherited by a person from his parents, and the property one gains through hard work are one's assets. Nobody wants to put such hard earnings in stakes and lose unless the person is really insane or foolish. Proverbs 6:6 reads,

"Go to the ant, thou sluggard; consider her ways, and be wise"   Lazy person loses money rather than increasing his wealth. Prudent men and women save money and increase in wealth and invest and increase money.

2 Thessalonians 3:10 reads, "For even when we

were with you, this we commanded you, that if any would not work, neither should he eat." It is true that if we do not work, we do not earn.

Prudent Christians also think in investing in God's work, which will certainly bring forth fruits that are pleasing to the Lord, and result in the expansion of the Kingdom of God. There is no doubt that we need to pay our attention to paying our bills and take care of our family needs. Let us also remember that it is God, who gave us health and wealth. He, therefore, deserves to be honored with our wealth.

We should, therefore, be careful when our minds wander in pursuit of earning money illegally. Jesus told us that no man can serve two masters as we read in Matthew 6:24,

"No man can serve two masters: for either he will hate the one, and love the other; or else he will hold to the one, and despise the other. Ye cannot serve God and mammon."

Any earning, which is not legal and that which comes to us as "quick-bucks" will not last for our good. Our desire to earn more money keeps increasing as we increase our pursuit for earning money and focus increases much on such endeavors. Now, let us also consider another point here.

Does investing in God's work a loss or gain? The contributions many pour out for God's work, such as establishing a church, or buying a church building, or spreading the gospel, or helping God's workers, are the good works for God that He never overlooks.

What do we gain amassing huge health and yet lose our health or lives? That was the question Jesus asked once. What if a man gain whole world and loses his own soul? Are we here on earth, only to eat, enjoy and amass wealth for ourselves and for our own children? Or, are we here to serve God while we live on this earth.

No doubt, our physical needs are to be met with. Nevertheless, we need to look after the needs of God's work as well.

Do we need to become millionaires on this earth? Actually, for a true Christian life is not a bed of roses. A Christian has to face innumerable challenges and tread the path of thorns.

The best way to become millionaire in heaven is to work for God or support the work of God. Each one has one's share of responsibility to partake in spreading the word of God. Jesus Christ said

"unless you remain in me, you can not do any thing". At another place He said, if we do not bear fruit for Him we are not worthy to be as branches of His body. Giving money for God's work is a great investing. God will never be our debtor.

We reap from our investments in Him the fruit that overflows our barns. When we cast our bread on waters we will surely find it.

"Cast thy bread upon the waters: for thou shalt find it after many days" (Ecclesiastes 11:1)

Nevertheless, when we owe to Him, we should never fail to give what we owed to Him. It is He who made heaven and the host there in. It is He who made the earth and all that is on it, and it is He who made seas and all that is therein. There is nothing that we can give to Him and boast that we gave something for Him to become millionaire. If we want to become millionaires in heaven, we need to work for Him and give to Him with whole heart. Please read Genesis 4th Chapter vs.3 to 5

"And in process of time it came to pass, that Cain brought of the fruit of the ground an offering unto the LORD. And Abel, he also brought of the firstlings of his flock and of the fat thereof. And the LORD had respect unto Abel and to his offering: But unto Cain and to his offering he had not respect. And Cain was very wroth, and his countenance fell" (Genesis 4:3-5)

We see here the difference between giving wholeheartedly and negligently. Abel brought fat portions from some of the first born of his flock; while Cain brought some of the fruits of the soil.

There is nothing like honoring God with our first fruits and giving pre-eminence to God in our lives. All that God demands from is honoring him, praising him, worshipping him. The attitude that we need to develop is to honor God. He needs something from the first, and not something from some that we have.

In Old Testament we read that we should not rob God of that belong to him, and we need to give to him tithe from our earnings.

"Will a man rob God? Yet ye have robbed me. But ye say, Wherein have we robbed thee? In tithes and offerings". (Malachi 3:8)

God says our barns will overflow if we honor him.

"Bring ye all the tithes into the storehouse, that there may be meat in mine house, and prove me now herewith, saith the LORD of hosts, if I will not open you the windows of heaven, and pour you out a blessing, that there shall not be room enough to receive it" (Malachi 3:10)

We do not find such a stringent asking in the New Testament. Yet, we read how Jesus honored a widow, who gave "all" that she had.

"For all these have of their abundance cast in unto the offerings of God: but she of her penury hath cast in all the living that she had" (Luke 21:4)

Jesus laid emphasis in our attitude of giving to God, what belongs to God, and give to Government, what belongs to Government. Jesus is asking us to give what belongs to God. The prominence should go to God.

The answer to the question "how to become millionaire" is simple. Do not think of become millionaire in this world; rather gather riches in heaven. Invest in Lord's work and give to God that which belongs to God, and test Him to see if He does not open heavens to see your barns overflow.

Apostle Paul writes that the message of the cross of Christ is foolishness to those, who are perishing, but to those who are saved it is the power of God.

When he came to know that there were contentions and divisions among the followers of Christ, and some of them identifying themselves as belonging to Apollos, and some to Cephas, and some to Christ, he questions them if Christ was divided? He further questions them if he (Paul) was crucified for them.

To the Jews the message of cross was not acceptable because they did not believe that Jesus bore our sins on the cross; rather they wanted to see signs and proofs. To the Greeks, who believed in philosophy and wisdom of this world, the message of cross was foolishness.

Paul's main motto was to preach the gospel of Jesus, "Who gave himself for our sins, that he might deliver us from this present evil world, according to the will of God and our Father" (Galatians 1:4) rather than baptizing. He laid emphasis on preaching 'Christ crucified' rather than usage of clever and attractive words, luring men into false confidence, and false promises of good health, or enough wealth, or guaranteed prosperous life.

Any other type of preaching without showing the truth of the cross where the Son of God shed his precious blood will be of no effect. Temporary assuage may be achieved by preaching resting on false promises, but sooner or later such preaching would be denounced.

God destroys the wise men of this world that treat the message of cross with contempt. Everything in this world is transient and temporary. What lasts is the eternal life that can be had only by faith in Jesus, who has paid price for our salvation. It is the gift of God and cannot be purchased with any amount of wealth of this world. (1 Corinthians 1:17-23)

Apostle Paul refers to two representatives of all humans in 1 Corinthians 15:45   And so it is written, The first man Adam was made a living soul; the last Adam was made a quickening spirit. Lord Jesus was fully man and fully divine.   Here in this verse, Paul refers to the human form of Jesus and calls him as the last Adam.   The first man on this earth, Adam, sinned and brought condemnation as heritage for everyone.

Condemnation is severe reproof, or accusation. In Adam everyone is condemned.   Added to that, we all commit sins.   Romans 3:23 says we all have sinned and come short of the glory of God.

Romans 6:23 says that 'the wages of sin is death; but the gift of God is eternal life through Jesus Christ our Lord'.

As we are all sinners, being the sons and daughters from Adam and Eve, who transgressed God's commandment, we deserved nothing but condemnation and judgment; but through the gift of grace that is given by Lord Jesus and having accepted this gift by faith in him, this condemnation and judgment are put away from us, and we are justified.

By 'the offence of one judgment came upon all

men to condemnation but the free gift is of many offences unto justification'. (Romans 5:18).

"There is therefore now no condemnation to them which are in Christ Jesus, who walk not after the flesh, but after the Spirit". Romans 8:1

The Scriptures say that if we say we have no sin, we not only deceive ourselves, but we make God a liar.

Therefore, everyone should accept before God that he has sinned and ask for forgiveness. The forgiveness is free from God, and there is no need to pay silver or Gold. The price is already paid by Jesus Christ on the cross of Calvary.

CHAPTER 11
THE RISEN LORD ASCENDED

And when he had spoken these things, while they beheld, he was taken up; and a cloud received him out of their sight. And while they looked stedfastly toward heaven as he went up, behold, two men stood by them in white apparel; Which also said, Ye men of Galilee, why stand ye gazing up into heaven? this same Jesus, which is taken up from you into heaven, shall so come in like manner as ye have seen him go into heaven. (Acts 1:9-11)

Judas Iscariot was already dead having committed suicide for betraying Jesus for crucifixion and after the resurrection of Lord Jesus Christ rest of the disciples numbering eleven went to Galilee at His instructions.   When the eleven disciples saw Lord Jesus Christ they worshipped Him, and yet there were some among them who did not believe that He was the risen Christ.

Jesus spoke to them saying that all power was given to Him in heaven and in earth and, thereafter, He commissioned them to go into all the nations baptizing them in the name of the

Father, the Son, and the Holy Spirit.   He also commanded them to teach the Word of God and to observe all the things that He had commanded them to do assuring that He will be with them always, even unto the end of world.

After Jesus gave them the authority to preach the Gospel of Jesus Christ he commanded them to assemble at Jerusalem and wait for the Promise of the Father to come upon them.   It was only after waiting at Jerusalem and receiving the Holy Spirit that they were supposed to preach the Gospel of Lord Jesus Christ.

The commandment to wait at Jerusalem and to receive the Holy Spirit was given to the disciples before the Holy Spirit came upon them.   After Holy Spirit came upon them they went   to preach the Gospel of Jesus Christ, first in Jerusalem, then in Judea and Samaria and then to the utter most part of the earth.

Holy Spirit has already come into this world and will be in the world for convicting and comforting and guiding the believers in Christ until Lord Jesus Christ comes again. He is the restrainer who reveals Antichrist in his due season and He will be no more in this world when Lord Jesus Christ appears in the clouds (cf. Luke 24:49, Acts 2:2-4, 1 Thessalonians 4:16-17 and 2 Thessalonians 2:6-7).

We the believers in Christ do not need to go to

Jerusalem or any other place to wait and receive the Holy Spirit. He is already here and whoever believes Lord Jesus Christ as personal Savior will receive Holy Spirit into his/her heart immediately. Holy Spirit indwells believer in Christ immediately a person is saved from his/her sins.

After giving the commandments Lord Jesus Christ ascended into heaven. From Acts 1;15 it is evident that Peter stood and in the midst of the disciples. The disciples included eleven who followed Jesus and Mathias who was chosen by lots in place of Judas Iscariot and others total one hundred and twenty initially. After He spoke these things and as they were watching a cloud received Him and He was out of their sight.

All of them witnessed risen Lord Jesus Christ ascending into heaven. He will come again just as He ascended into heaven. Lord Jesus Christ showed Himself after His passion by infallible proofs and was seen for forty days before He was taken out of their sight.

To whom also he shewed himself alive after his passion by many infallible proofs, being seen of them forty days, and speaking of the things pertaining to the kingdom of God: (Acts 1:3)

FORGIVING ONE ANOTHER

"Then said Jesus, Father, forgive them; for they know not what they do. And they parted his raiment, and cast lots" (Luke 23:34)

In the early days after the ascension of Lord Jesus Christ, when Apostles started working for the proclamation of Gospel of Jesus Christ the power of God was clearly seen when multitude of people were saved. In Acts 2nd Chapter this fact can be seen.

Apostle Peter spoke about repentance and remission of sins and there were three thousand souls were added. And they continued steadfastly in the "apostles' doctrine and fellowship, and in breaking of bread, and in prayers". (Acts 2:42)

The Church grew and the twelve disciples of Jesus [Matthias was appointed in place of Judas Iscariot (Acts 1:26)] were convinced of the fact that they should devote more time and energy for the purpose of serving God rather than pursuing secular interests.

It was then that they took a decision to appoint seven men with honest report, filled with Holy Spirit and wisdom to do this job. Their decision was in consequence to their willingness to dedicate their entire time and energy for prayer and for the ministry of the Word of God.

Of the seven men they chose for this work ["Stephen, a man full of faith and of the Holy Ghost, and Philip, and Prochorus, and Nicanor, and Timon, and Parmenas, and Nicolas a proselyte of Antioch" (Acts 6:5)] Stephen deserves more of our attention than others.

Stephen was the first martyr who gave up his mortal life for the sake of proclaiming the saving grace of Lord Jesus Christ, who was the Son of God. Jesus came into this world for taking upon Himself our sins and die on behalf of us, in order that whoever believes on him shall not perish but have everlasting life.

The multitude of people stoned Stephen to death for standing for Jesus Christ. "And they stoned Stephen, calling upon God, and saying, Lord Jesus, receive my spirit" (Acts 7:59)

While breathing his last, Stephen knelt down and "cried with a loud voice, Lord, lay not this sin to their charge. And when he had said this, he fell asleep". (Acts 7:60)

Peter and John, the disciples of Jesus Christ, preached the Gospel and the resurrection from the dead. They healed an impotent man in the name of Jesus. Their ministry was blessed and the number of believers increased from three thousand to five thousand. This kind of preaching, and miracles, in the name of Jesus, grieved the high priest Annas, Caiphas, John, and Alexander, who thought that the preaching belonged to them, and there is no resurrection from the dead.

The Pharisees and Sadducees did not believe in the resurrection, and as they were against this teaching they laid hands on Peter and John, the disciples of Jesus, for a trial the next day. The elders, scribes, Annas, the high priest and high priest's kindred gathered at Jerusalem and questioned the authority by which they healed the impotent man, and preached the resurrection from the dead.

Peter, then, filled with Holy Spirit, spoke to them and said to them very firmly that they preached and healed the impotent man in the name of Jesus Christ of Nazareth, whom they crucified, and whom God raised from the dead.

Jesus is the stone, who these elders, Pharisees, Sadducees rejected, but God set him as the Chief corner stone. David prophesied about Jesus, who was the stone, that the builders rejected, yet the LORD made him the head stone of the corner.

Peter and John, the disciples of Jesus, who walked with him, witnessed that Jesus was the stone, whom the Jews rejected, but he became the head stone of the corner. They affirm that there is no other name under heaven where anyone can find salvation.

One may object to this preaching but the Bible says it very firmly that there is no salvation except by believing that Jesus is the Savior. Peter and John, the Apostles, who were not learned, or educated, boldly said these things because they were with Jesus and took knowledge from him, who is the only begotten Son of God. The accusers attempted to execute the disciples of Jesus but did not find any cause to punish them, and let them go.

Acts 4:1-14, Psalm 118:21-23. Isaiah 28:16, Ro 9:33, Ephesians 2:20, 1Pe 2:7

CHAPTER 12
REPLIES BY ADAM AND CAIN

ADAM'S REPLY

"And the LORD God called unto Adam, and said unto him, Where art thou? And he said, I heard thy voice in the garden, and I was afraid, because I was naked; and I hid myself" (Genesis 3:9-10) Even though the ground was cursed for man he was forgiven of his transgression when God himself covered the nakedness of Adam and Eve with coats of skin. The skin was not obtainable unless an animal was killed. Who killed the animal for their sake, then? Obviously God himself killed the animal as sacrifice for the sake of Adam and Eve and clothed them with righteousness. This also showed how the Son of God was to be killed in the stead of man for redeeming man from the bondage of sin. This was fulfilled in Jesus who was crucified on the cross for our sake.

"Unto Adam also and to his wife did the LORD God make coats of skins, and clothed them". (Genesis 3:21)

CAIN'S REPLY:

"And the LORD said unto Cain, Where is Abel thy brother? And he said, I know not: Am I my brother's keeper?" (Genesis 4:9)

Cain's irresponsible, arrogant, rude reply to the Almighty God invited curse for himself. If only Cain were to be as humble as his father was he would have surely been forgiven of his sin. Cain chose his way and his way led him to destruction. There is no sin, except blasphemy of Holy Spirit, that cannot be forgiven. Every sin is pardonable. God is kind and loving and he is inviting even now every sinner to humble and repent of sins.

GOD SAID

"When thou tillest the ground, it shall not henceforth yield unto thee her strength; a fugitive and a vagabond shalt thou be in the earth". (Genesis 4:12)

Cain said to God that his punishment was greater than he could bear and anyone finding him shall slay him. But then God said whoever kills Cain will be punished seven-fold and He set a mark upon Cain in order that no one may kill him. That is to say Cain will run fugitive and be vagabond entire his life.

In spite of that severe curse God did not allow Cain to live like a beggar. It was not Satan's way of redeeming Cain from that severe curse for him to build a city or to have possessions, but it was God's way of leaving Cain out to his own choices. Satan is a liar and cheat. Satan will deceive even those who worship him. God will cast Satan and his followers along with death and hell in to 'lake of fire' (Revelation 19:20, 20:10-15).

Cain never repented but he continued to be rebellious and led his life of arrogant attitude. Cain's acquiring wealth showed his attitude of pride that he could live without God's help in spite of the curse on him.

Let us see what it means to say "Fugitive" and "Vagabond".

'FUGITIVE'

Hebrew Strong's number 5128. nuwa` means to go up and down, be gone away, be moveable, be removed, be scattered etc.

This word was used as 'removed' in Exodus 20:18, as 'wander' in Numbers 32:13, as 'moved' in1 Samuel 1:13, as 'hath shaken' in 2 Kings 19:21, as 'scatter' in Psalms 59:11 and many more with similar meanings.

'VAGABOND'

Hebrew Strong's number 5110. nuwd means: waver; figuratively, to wander, flee, disappear;

This word was used as "is shaken" in 1 Kings 14:15, as "to mourn" in Job 2:11, as "for some to take pity" in Psalms 69:20 and many more with similar meanings.

Going by the meaning of these words the curse does not mean Cain would have become a beggar. Cain went from the presence of the Lord and dwelt in the land of Nod, on the east of Eden. If these words had any other meaning than that those Hebrew Strong's numbers presented, God would not have allowed Cain to have wife. But then Cain had a wife and he knew his wife and she conceived. She bore Cain Enoch and Cain built a city and called the name of the city Enoch after the name of his son. (Genesis 4:15-17)

CHAPTER 13
CAIN AND HIS CURSE

After Adam and Eve were driven out from the garden of Eden, God "placed at the east of the garden of Eden Cherubims, and a flaming sword which turned every way, to keep the tree of life" (Genesis 3:24)

Thereafter Adam knew his wife and she bore him a son and that son was called by the name "Cain". There is no reason to believe that Adam did not "know" Eve before he fell from the presence of the Lord, but this is about his "Knowing" his wife after his transgression.

"And God blessed them, and God said unto them, Be fruitful, and multiply, and replenish the earth, and subdue it: and have dominion over the fish of the sea, and over the fowl of the air, and over every living thing that moveth upon the earth". Genesis 1:28

Eve said she got a man from the LORD. Eve heard earlier curse from God on the serpent. God said:

"And I will put enmity between thee and the woman, and between thy seed and her seed; it shall bruise thy head, and thou shalt bruise his

heel." Genesis 3:15

Eve probably thought Cain was the savior, but alas! he turned out to be a killer, satanic perfect portrait. Eve bore another son and the son was called by the name "Abel". Cain was tiller of the ground and Abel was keeper of sheep. The ground was already cursed by then because Adam and Eve transgressed God's command and God cursed the ground for man.

Cain undertook hard part of the work and bore much of results of the curse already by then. Abel was a keeper of sheep. A Shepherd keeps his sheep risking his own life against the possibility of getting killed. If one sheep is lost its way the Shepherd leaves behind other sheep in search of the lost sheep and when he finds it he rejoices. This shows that Abel held great responsibility of keeping the sheep and protecting them.

Cain and Abel brought their offerings to the LORD. Obviously they both felt the need of honoring God with offerings. It was God's choice to accept or reject one or both the offerings.

Yet, God did not reject any offering but showed his displeasure in Cain's offering and pleasure in Abel's offering. Cain brought of the first fruit of the ground and of the fat thereof. Cain had the hard part of the work and he worked hard and brought the first fruit of the ground and in addition of the fat thereof.

Abel brought the firstlings of his flock and the fat thereof. It was God's prerogative which offering to accept or which one to reject or accept both or reject both.

It was not rather a competitive offering but each one offered offering that he thought would be pleasing to the LORD. God had respect unto Abel and to his offering but unto Cain and to his offering he had not respect.

Scripture does not say Cain's offering was rejected but it says God had respect unto Abel's offering. Cain was very angry and his happiness on his face and in heart fell. The LORD asked Cain as to why his countenance has fallen. God also asked Cain that if Cain did well would he not have been accepted. But Cain did badly and sin was at his door.

By this time Cain had already killed his brother Abel. If Cain did well he would have ruled over sin. But this did not happen. Cain became subservient to sin and sin ruled over him.

Some ask if there was any way Cain could circumvent the curse announced on him by God. The possibilities, perhaps, could be to fly to "Jupiter" or "Saturn" from earth to get off the curse or, perhaps, he could have hidden in a submarine whole of his life!

No, there was no way Cain could get out of the curse announced by God unless God himself forgave him if Cain repented. God's approach to Cain was very pleasing and loving when He asked Cain if he could ask forgiveness; yet Cain chose his way.

"If thou doest well, shalt thou not be accepted? and if thou doest not well, sin lieth at the door. And unto thee shall be his desire, and thou shalt rule over him". (Genesis 4:7)

"Men in the end days seek death but they will not find it; they desire to die and death will flee from them" (Revelation 9:6).

There is only one way to find peace with God and receive forgiveness from him. It is by faith in Jesus that He is the Son of God and repenting from past sins. There is no other way anyone could escape the wrath announced on man.

Believe that Jesus is the way, the truth, and the life. No man can come to the Father without Jesus.

"Jesus saith unto him, I am the way, the truth, and the life: no man cometh unto the Father, but by me". (John 14:6)

From Hebrews 11:4 we understand that God desired animal sacrifice. Abel offered more excellent offering than that of Cain. God showed that his pleasure in Abel's offering was because blood was shed. Abel's offering was a shadow of the things to be fulfilled in Lord Jesus Christ, whose blood was shed for cleansing us from our sins.

Jesus died on the cross for the remission of our sins. Whoever believes that Jesus is the savior will have eternal life. Abel obtained witness that he was righteous. God testified of the gifts of Abel even though he was dead, yet his offering spoke of his heart.

"By faith Abel offered unto God a more excellent sacrifice than Cain, by which he obtained witness that he was righteous, God testifying of his gifts: and by it he being dead yet speaketh". (Hebrews 11:4)

Cain killed Abel his brother in the field and gave a very irresponsible answer to God when God asked him where Abel was.

"And the LORD said unto Cain, Where is Abel thy brother? And he said, I know not: Am I my brother's keeper?" (Genesis 4:9)

If Cain had asked forgiveness surely he would have been forgiven, but he chose not to ask forgiveness but he countered God with an arrogant question in response to God's question. That made all the difference.

Satan thought he could become greater than God but he was thrown out from his eminence as the chief of angels. No less was the attitude of Cain when retorted God with an arrogant question if he was keeper of his brother.

God said to Cain that his Brother Abel's blood cried from the ground and God cursed Cain. Cain's curse was too much for him to bear and he desired that anyone finding him going as fugitive and vagabond would kill him. (Genesis 4:11-13)

WHERE DID CAIN GET HIS WIFE FROM?

Cain and Abel were the sons of Adam and Eve. Cain killed Abel, and thereafter, there were no women to Adam and Eve, until they bore children, male and female. Obviously Cain's wife was his sister from Adam and Eve. Before the law was given to Moses God permitted such marriages. Abraham also married his half-sister. It was not counted as sin. But the wickedness such as was prevalent just before Noah's period and in Sodom and Gomorrah were intolerable in the sight of God.

Seth's sons and Cain's daughters intermarried and the result was flood over the face of the earth for forty days and forty nights during the days of Noah, who with his family members and certain chosen fowl, cattle, and creeping things were spared from the wrath of God. The wickedness during Lot's period in Sodom and Gomorrah was intolerable.

Besides the wickedness which in God's sight was intolerable, there were those who wanted to lay with angels, who were in the form of men, and God struck the offenders with blindness and the cities with fire and brimstone, while Lot was saved from the wrath.

Cain did not repent any time from the time his offering was not accepted. Cain gave an arrogant and rude reply to God. Cain went from the presence of the Lord and remained fugitive and vagabond, restless, never enjoying what he could possess or build. The possessions and buildings were not denied to him. Cain chose his way and remained restless.

Cain's name figures three times in the New Testament.

Firstly it is in Hebrews 11:4

"By faith Abel offered unto God a more excellent sacrifice than Cain, by which he obtained witness that he was righteous, God testifying of his gifts: and by it he being dead yet speaketh"

God desired animal sacrifice as we read in Hebrew 11:4 in preference to any other offering and that was a shadow of the things to be fulfilled in Jesus Christ.

Earlier, God clothed Adam and Eve with coats of skin signifying that it is necessary that blood had to shed for the remission of sins and sin has to be covered. Jesus Christ died for our sake on the cross becoming our Passover lamb.

He was buried and rose from the dead on the third day and after appearing to many for forty days he ascended into heaven. Jesus will come back in the same way he ascended into heaven.

Secondly in 1John 3:12

"Not as Cain, who was of that wicked one, and slew his brother. And wherefore slew he him? Because his own works were evil, and his brother's righteous"

If we look at the context where this verse appears we see that it deals with the brotherly love. Scripture says here that one should love another not as Cain showed his wickedness.

Because Cain's works were of evil he killed his brother. If we take this a step forward we see that Cain's reply was very arrogant and rude to the Almighty God. Instead of repenting of what he had done Cain countered God with a question if he was his brother's keeper.

There was absolutely no remorse on the part of Cain on his evil works but he was unrepentant and also turned away from the Lord. For a willful sinner there remains no sacrifice for sins.

It was not about the Saved one that Hebrews 10:26 spoke but of the unsaved one who sins willfully after receiving the knowledge of the truth that there remains no more sacrifice.

"For if we sin wilfully after that we have received the knowledge of the truth, there remaineth no more sacrifice for sins" (Hebrews 10:26)

Cain saw his parents were pardoned although they were driven out from the Garden of Eden, yet their salvation was not lost. But Cain blatantly refused to tread the path of righteousness and repentance.

That is why he was wandering like a fugitive and vagabond, yet not like a beggar but could build city. It was his earthly abode where he lived and wandered without rest. He possessed yet not enjoyed any of his possessions. He lived but did not live happily.

Thirdly in Jude 1:11

"Woe unto them! for they have gone in the way of Cain, and ran greedily after the error of Balaam for reward, and perished in the gainsaying of Core"

Jude, the servant of Jesus Christ, and brother of James, wrote about false teachers and said that they had gone in the way of Cain, showing unrighteousness, rebellion, and disobedience and also desired of gaining wealth and power just as Balaam tried to gain, but perished. God calls those unrepentant to repent and turn to Jesus for forgiveness of their sins.

"Behold, I stand at the door, and knock: if any man hear my voice, and open the door, I will come in to him, and will sup with him, and he with me" (Revelation 3:20)

CHAPTER 14
STREET OF GOLD

In this secular world we see the importance of gold and other precious metals, which are possessed by only affluent people. The poor cannot afford to have them. One of the precious metals most people like is gold, while the other precious metals are practically unreachable to the common man.

What if we are, the common people in this world can tread on a street of gold, and live in a city made of the most precious metals? Bible speaks of such precious metals, which even common man tread on, and live in a city made of most precious metals.

Revelation chapter 21 presents the most beautiful city and the inhabitants there in. The revelation was given by Jesus Christ to John, so that we can read and understand what is in store for us. It was a new earth and a new heaven that John saw in his divine vision, in which a great revelation by Jesus was presented to John and through him to us.

John saw in his vision the holy city, New Jerusalem, coming down out of heaven from God, prepared for a bride, who was adorned for her husband.   The description is great.

Who is this bride?   Bible speaks of the bride as the Church/Assembly constituting the believers in Christ, the saved ones.   The bride is adorned waiting for her husband to come and here is the chaste virgin, adorned waiting for the New Jerusalem.

The tabernacle is referred to in the Old Testament, as the sacred tent in which God came and dwelt. Here in this chapter John saw God himself coming down and dwelling among his people, who will be his people, and he will be their God, who will wipe away all their tears, and there will be no more death, nor sorrow, nor crying, no more pain, because all the old things have passed away by them.

It is the new heaven where the Assembly/Church, constituting the saved ones, which is his bride, will dwell. Isaiah 65:17 presents the prophecy about the new heavens and a new earth that will be created and about the former earth and heaven which will pass away and will not be remembered. In Revelation 21:1 we read that city, which is beautiful and which has no sea, but only the inhabitants, who are always happy and without any sufferings.

Jesus is the Alpha and Omega, the Beginning and

the End, and he is the one, who gives fountain of the water of life freely to him, who thirsts. He, who overcomes shall inherit all things, and Jesus will be his God and he will be His son.

This chapter also speaks of others, who are not his children that are cowards, unbelievers, abominable, murderers, sexually immoral, sorcerers, idolaters, and liars, who will have their part and living in the lake, which burns with fire and brimstone, and that is their second death.

There is no second death for the believers. There is only happiness and their dwelling will be in a city made of precious metals, and whose street is made of gold.

John was carried in spirit by one of the seven angels, who came to him and talked to him, and asked him to accompany him to see the bride, which is the wife of the Lamb.

Jesus was called as the 'lamb of God' in the Gospel of John, and the believers in Jesus Christ are his bride.

John was carried in spirit to a high mountain and was shown the great city, the holy Jerusalem, descending out of heaven from God, having the glory of God. The light of the city was like that of most precious stone, the Japer stone, and clear as crystal.

The city had great and high wall with twelve gates, and twelve angels at the twelve gates, and names of the twelve tribes of the children of Israel, written on the gates.   The city has three gates on the east, three gates on the north, three gates on the south, and three gates on the west. The wall of the city had twelve foundations, where the names of the twelve apostles of the Lamb, were written.

After measuring the wall as directed by the angel, John saw that the construction of the wall of the city was of Jasper, and the city was pure gold, like clear glass.

The foundations of the wall of the city were adorned with all kinds of precious stones; the first foundation was Jasper, the second sapphire, the third chalcedony, the fourth emerald, the fifth sardonyx, the sixth sardius, the seventh chrysolite, the eighth beryl, the ninth topaz, the tenth chrysoprase, the eleventh jacinth, and the twelfth amethyst.

The twelve gates were twelve pearls and each individual gate was of one pearl.   The street of the city was pure gold, like transparent glass.

There was no temple in it, because, God the Lord Almighty and the Lamb are its temple.   There was no necessity for Sun or Moon to be there because the glory of the God illuminated the city.

"And I saw no temple therein: for the Lord God Almighty and the Lamb are the temple of it. And the city had no need of the sun, neither of the moon, to shine in it: for the glory of God did lighten it, and the Lamb is the light thereof"

In the beginning God called light into existence and He saw that the light was good and God divided light from darkness.

"And God saw the light, that it was good: and God divided the light from the darkness. And God called the light Day, and the darkness he called Night. And the evening and the morning were the first day. (Genesis 1:4-5)"

On the fourth day of creation God made two great lights - the greater to rule the day and the lesser to rule the night and He made stars also. We know them by 'sun' and 'moon'.

These two lights were created to divide day from night and let them be for signs and for seasons and for days and years. In eternity we do not need such divisions.

New Jerusalem where we dwell does not need sun and moon to shine in it because the glory of God that shines in it is greater than any light.

The Lamb of God, who is our Lord Jesus Christ, is the light in it. "And God said, Let there be lights in the firmament of the heaven to divide the day from the night; and let them be for signs, and for seasons, and for days, and years" (Genesis 1:14)

"And the city had no need of the sun, neither of the moon, to shine in it: for the glory of God did lighten it, and the Lamb is the light thereof" (Revelation 21:23)

"And there shall be no night there; and they need no candle, neither light of the sun; for the Lord God giveth them light: and they shall reign for ever and ever. (Revelation 22:5)"

All the nations saved through the blood of Jesus Christ, the lamb of God, will walk in its light and the kings of the earth bring their glory and honor in to it.

The gates of that city will never be shut by day and there shall be no night.   The kings of earth shall bring the honor of the nations into it.

Final words in this chapter have important point, which says that, 'there shall by no means enter in anything that defiles, or causes an abomination or a lie, but only those who are written in the Lamb's Book of Life.

Lord Jesus Christ has undergone severe pain when men pierced sword in to his body and beat him. He was crowned with a crown of thorns and blood and water gushed forth from the side of his body.

It is through that blood of Jesus Christ that we are saved. He suffered on the cross of Calvary that so that we may have eternal life. It is through the shedding of his precious blood that our sins are cleansed and through that blood our filth is cleaned and we are clear as crystal.

That city of precious metals is prepared for us. Vs. 18 "And the building of the wall of it was of jasper: and the city was pure gold, like unto clear glass."

But for those who do not accept Jesus Christ as their personal Savior, there is another place, which the lake of fire, as we read in vs. 8   That is the place, the "lake which burneth with fire and brimstone: which is the second death."

Many are heading to that place knowingly. The cowards, who are afraid of proclaiming Jesus as the Savior, are the leaders in this line. The ones who have committed sins namely, murder, adultery, sorcery, idolatry, and lying will follow these cowards.

The punishment laid down for them is terrible. They have their part in the lake that burns with fire and brimstone, which is the second death. We would like to have our names written in the Lamb's book of life. It would be terrible if our names are not found there.

MOSES WARNED

"I call heaven and earth to record this day against you, that I have set before you life and death, blessing and cursing: therefore choose life that both thou and thy seed may live" Deuteronomy 30":19

Apostle Paul wrote...

"For the wages of sin is death; but the gift of God is eternal life through Jesus Christ our Lord."

Yes! Indeed,

"For God so loved the world, that he gave his only begotten Son, that whosoever believeth in him should not perish, but have everlasting life"

Let us introspect what is our state today. Are we like the ones who enter the city with street of gold and transparent glasses and all the precious stones on its walls, or, are we like the ones who are afraid of proclaiming Jesus Christ as the Savior of the world and heading towards lake of fire that has fire and brimstone in it. The final words are very severe in nature.

And there shall in no wise enter into it anything that defileth, neither whatsoever worketh abomination, or maketh a lie: but they which are written in the Lamb's book of life." Revelation 21:27.

Please accept Jesus Christ as your personal Savior today. Today is the day of salvation.

CHRISTIAN SOLDIER
Spiritual warfare

LESLIE M. JOHN

www.ingramcontent.com/pod-product-compliance
Lightning Source LLC
Chambersburg PA
CBHW071457040426
42444CB00008B/1386